Grateful thanks to Matt McKay for conceiving and organizing this project; and to Carole Honeychurch for a thorough and skillful job in editing the manuscript.

Finally I am indebted to my partner, Jane, for her support, encouragement, and for carefully processing several drafts of the text.

OVERCOMING SPECIFIC PHOBIA

■

A Hierarchy and
Exposure–Based Protocol
for the Treatment
of All Specific Phobias

Edmund J. Bourne, Ph.D.

Distributed in the U.S.A. by Publisher's Group West; in Canada by Raincoast Books; in Great Britain by Airlift Book Company, Ltd.; in South Africa by Real Books, Ltd.; in Australia by Boobook; and in New Zealand by Tandem Press.

Copyright © 1998 by Edmund J. Bourne, Ph.D.
New Harbinger Publications, Inc.
5674 Shattuck Avenue
Oakland, CA 94609

Cover design by Poulson/Gluck Design.
Edited by Carole Honeychurch.
Text design by Michele Waters.

ISBN 1-57224-114-4 Paperback

New Harbinger Publications' Website address: www.newharbinger.com

First Printing

Contents

Specific Phobia—A Brief Overview

Specific phobia can be defined as a strong *fear and avoidance of one particular type of object or situation*. This kind of fear is not only intense, it is nearly always irrational. You may be able to ski mountains or speak in front of people easily, yet you might have an irrational fear of riding in elevators or getting an injection. If you are an adult, you always recognize the phobia to be irrational (this is not necessarily true for children with specific phobias).

With specific phobia, you may panic if forced to confront your phobic situation, but you do not otherwise have panic attacks. Also, you do not have unreasonable anxiety in social or interpersonal situations such as meetings, classrooms, or gatherings, which would constitute what is called *social phobia*. To receive a diagnosis of specific phobia, your particular fear has to create problems for you. It may interfere with your normal routines, your work, your social relationships, and/or it may cause you significant distress. Even though you recognize your fear's irrationality, you cannot will it away.

Specific phobias are common and affect approximately 10 percent of the population. Usually they begin in adolescence or adulthood, although sometimes they are carryovers from childhood. They can begin suddenly and tend to persist longer than childhood fears; only 20 percent of adult phobias go away on their own. If the object of the phobia is easy to avoid and does not disrupt their daily life, people with specific phobia often choose not to seek treatment. Women are slightly more inclined to have specific phobias than men, although this statistic may be due to the tendency of women to seek treatment more often than men.

Among the most common specific phobias are the following:

Animal phobias. These can include fear and avoidance of snakes, bats, rats, spiders, bees, dogs, and other creatures. Often these phobias begin in childhood, where they are usually considered normal fears, although they may be treated. When they persist into adulthood and disrupt your life or cause significant distress they are always classified as specific phobias.

Acrophobia (fear of heights). With acrophobia, you tend to be afraid of high floors of buildings or of finding yourself atop mountains, hills, or high-level bridges. In such situations you may experience: 1) vertigo (dizziness) or 2) an urge to jump, usually experienced as some external force drawing you to the edge.

Elevator phobia. This phobia usually involves a fear that the elevator will get stuck and you will be trapped inside. You may have panic reactions in response to being in an elevator but you have no history of panic attacks otherwise.

Airplane phobia. This most often involves a fear that the plane will crash. Alternatively, it can involve a fear of being confined for a period of time without the ability to exit. More recently, phobias about planes being hijacked or bombed have become common. When flying, you may have a panic attack. Apart from flying, you have no history of panic attacks. Fear of flying is a very common phobia. Approximately 10 percent of the population will not fly at all, while an additional 20 percent experience considerable anxiety while flying.

Doctor or dentist phobias. This can begin as a fear of painful procedures (injections, having teeth filled) conducted in a doctor's or dentist's office. Later it can generalize to anything having to do with doctors or dentists. The danger is that you may avoid needed medical treatment.

Blood-injury phobia. This is a unique phobia in that you have a tendency to faint (rather than panic) if exposed to blood or your own pain through injections or inadvertent injury. People with blood-injury phobia tend to be both physically and psychologically healthy in other regards.

Natural environment phobias. This category includes fears of water, fire, or natural disasters such as tornadoes or earthquakes. It also includes the fear of thunder and lightning. Many such fears begin in childhood and, without treatment, they may persist into adulthood. Such fears can also develop in the aftermath of a frightening encounter with a natural disaster.

Situational phobias. In addition to the fears of flying and of elevators, a specific phobia can develop in response to any situation that might cause a person to feel confined, such as public transportation, tunnels, bridges, driving on freeways, or being in a movie theater. Generally, you are only afraid of one particular type of situation and do not have a history of spontaneous panic attacks or multiple phobias (this would be a different anxiety disorder, called *agoraphobia*).

Illness phobia. Usually this phobia involves a fear of contracting and/or ultimately succumbing to a specific illness, such as a heart attack or cancer. With illness phobias you tend to seek constant reassurance from doctors and will avoid any situation that reminds you of the dreaded disease. Illness phobia is different from *hypochondria*, where you tend to imagine you already have different types of diseases rather than fearing you will contract one in particular.

As previously mentioned, specific phobias are often childhood fears that were never outgrown. In other instances they may develop after a traumatic event, such as an accident, natural disaster, illness, or visit to the dentist—in other words, as a result of *conditioning*. Conditioning means you unconsciously associate anxiety with a particular situation that caused you distress. Subsequent exposure to that situation automatically evokes a response of further anxiety. A final cause of phobias is childhood *modeling*. Repeated observation of a parent with a specific phobia can lead a child to develop it as well.

Specific phobias tend to be easier to treat than other types of anxiety disorders since they do not involve spontaneous panic attacks or multiple phobias. They can often be treated without medication and in a fairly short period of time. The treatment of choice for specific phobias is *cognitive behavioral therapy emphasizing graded exposure*, which often succeeds in alleviating the problem (see the next section). Approximately 80 percent of persons with specific phobia can be helped by this kind of therapy.

To sum up, specific phobia is usually a benign disorder, particularly if it begins as a common childhood fear. Though it may last for years, it rarely gets worse and often diminishes over time. Typically it is not associated with other psychiatric disturbances. People with specific phobias are usually functioning at a high level in other respects. The treatment for specific phobia is straightforward and usually effective, provided you are motivated to overcome the problem and cooperate with the treatment process.

Treatment Approaches

Up until the 1960s phobias were treated primarily through insight-oriented therapy, which seeks to uncover the origin of a phobia in childhood trauma. Insight therapy was not particularly effective; understanding the causes of phobia in the past doesn't necessarily change your fear of a particular situation or habit of avoiding it.

The first effective treatment for phobias was *systematic desensitization*, developed by a South African psychiatrist, Joseph Wolpe, in the late 1950s. Systematic desensitization combines relaxation with a structured process of gradually confronting a phobic object or situation, most often in imagery, although sometimes in real life. You would be asked to visualize a series of scenes relating to your phobia, which gradually increase in their fear-evoking potential. For example, in the case of phobia of injections, you might start off visualizing a doctor's office, followed by a scene of someone else getting a shot, and concluding with a scene where you picture yourself receiving a shot. Or if you were afraid of snakes, you would start by looking at pictures of snakes, then visualize yourself in the presence of a snake, then see yourself handling a snake, then approach a toy snake, and finally visit a zoo where you would witness and/or handle live snakes. Usually there are eight to twenty scenes or situations which gradually increase in intensity, what Wolpe called a "stimulus hierarchy." You visualize each scene (or face each situation) in a relaxed state until you habituate or "desensitize" to it; then you proceed to the next scene in the hierarchy. After completing desensitization to all of the scenes or situations, you are better able to face your phobic situation with little or no anxiety.

Wolpe found that direct exposure to a phobic object or situation in real life was particularly effective for animal phobias of dogs, insects, or snakes. During the 1970s real-life desensitization came to be used increasingly in conjunction with or in lieu of systematic (imagery) desensitization. What came to be called "exposure therapy" or simply *exposure,* has been the dominant method of treatment for phobias since that time. Imagery desensitization is still used primarily in the case of phobias that don't lend themselves to direct exposure. For example, if you fear a natural disaster such as a tornado or earthquake, it is hard to simulate real-life exposures, so it's necessary to do the exposures in imagery. However for most phobias, whether of heights, flying, driving freeways, injections, elevators, or water, progressive exposure is the treatment of choice. To do exposure, you first define a hierarchy of incremental confrontations with your phobic object or situation in real life. Then you gradually work through these confrontations, usually having your therapist or a support person accompany you. You habituate to each step in your hierarchy before going on to the next one. (An example of a typical exposure hierarchy is provided in the next section.)

Research over the past twenty years supports the efficacy of exposure in treating phobias. Nothing works better in overcoming a phobia than to face it. Exposure is effective because it allows you to face what you fear in a manageable and relatively comfortable way—through a series of small, incremental steps.

About This Treatment Program

This treatment program for overcoming your phobia will take place over ten weekly sessions. Here is a brief outline:

1. Initial evaluation

2. Abdominal breathing and relaxation training

3. Overcoming negative self-talk that contributes to your fear

4. Anxiety/worry coping skills

5. Imagery desensitization (visualizing your phobic situation)

6. Exposure—setting up your exposure hierarchy

7–9. Exposure practice

10. Review, closure, and planning follow-up.

Ten weekly sessions is the minimum time needed for you to learn and practice the skills necessary to overcome your phobia. It may, in fact, take more than ten weeks for you to fully master your fear. However, you will have learned enough about how to do exposure by the end of ten weeks so that you can continue on your own afterward, if necessary. Your therapist may continue to work with you beyond ten sessions. If this is impractical, she or he will certainly be available to you by phone if you need assistance while conducting your own exposure.

As you can see, the treatment approach adopted here is primarily *educational*, requiring that you learn and practice certain skills. Your therapist will not spend much time exploring possible causes of your phobia in the past. Research has demonstrated that such an approach is not particularly helpful. Instead, you will *learn* particular skills that enable you to face and overcome your fear, and you will *unlearn* conditioned patterns of thinking, feeling, and acting that perpetuate your phobia. The term for this treatment approach is cognitive-behavioral therapy. Nearly all therapists who treat phobias these days employ such an approach.

The outline above explains the progression of treatment. During the first session your therapist will do a thorough evaluation of your particular situation so she or he can tailor the therapy to your unique needs. This evaluation includes filling out the Fear Questionnaire to gauge the severity of your symptoms. In Session 2, you will learn breathing and relaxation techniques that will enable you to reduce feelings of anxiety at the moment they occur. If you practice these skills on a regular basis, you should become proficient in being able to reduce anxiety or worry that come up in connection with your phobia.

Session 3 focuses on helping you to identify and eliminate unproductive thinking which contributes to your fear. When you think about facing your fear, you probably start to get anxious. That anxiety, called *anticipatory anxiety,* is mostly due to unhelpful, frightening thoughts you have about your phobia. Usually there are two kinds of anxiety-provoking thoughts. First, there are those which *overestimate the odds of something undesirable happening* when you face your fear. These overestimating thoughts often begin with a "What if. . . ," for example: "What if I panic and feel trapped on the plane," "What if I faint while getting a shot," or "What if the elevator stops between floors and I'm trapped?" The other kind of unhelpful thoughts are those where you *underestimate your ability to cope* with your phobic situation, for example: "There is no way I can ever do that," or "If I panicked, I'd be at a total loss about what to do." You can learn to recognize, challenge, and counter unhelpful self-talk. After a while, this will help you to change your attitude—the way you look at—facing your phobia.

In session 4 you will learn helpful strategies and skills for minimizing anxiety that might come up when you begin to actually confront your fear in real life. In addition to the breathing techniques taught in session 2, you will learn to use coping statements such as "I can handle this" and other useful distraction techniques to limit anxiety symptoms as they occur. With these skills in place, you'll find you're more confident and at ease about actually facing your fear.

In session 5 you will learn how to do imagery desensitization. Before facing your fear in real life, you will face it in imagery. You will practice visualizing yourself confronting what you fear through a series of incremental steps. This, too, will help make real-life exposure to your phobic situation easier.

The heart of this therapy program is the real-life exposure you will learn and practice in sessions 6–9. Exposure will require some commitment and effort on your part, but it is by far the most effective treatment for your phobia. It's true that you may experience some anxiety when you begin to face a situation you've been avoiding for a long time. This is normal and to be expected. However, the anxiety you feel is likely to be less than you might think, for several reasons. First, you will have learned and mastered a number of anxiety management skills that will enable you to handle any anxiety that comes up. Second, you will have your therapist and/or a support person (usually a close friend or family member) accompanying you. Having someone go with you while you face your phobia provides both support and distraction and will help increase your confidence. Eventually, you will learn to face your phobia without a support person; but, in the early stages of exposure, it's good to have such a person with you. Finally, recall that exposure involves breaking down the process of facing your fear into a series of small, manageable steps. You will learn to habituate to each step in your hierarchy before going on to the next. An example of a phobia hierarchy, relevant to a fear of elevators, would look something like this:

1. Look at elevators, watching them come and go.

2. Stand in a stationary elevator with your support person.

3. Travel up or down one floor with your support person.

4. Travel two to three floors with your support person.

5. Stand in a stationary elevator alone.

6. Travel up or down one floor alone, with your support person waiting outside the elevator on the floor where you will arrive.

7. Travel two to three floors alone, with your support person waiting outside the elevator on the floor where you will arrive.

8. Extend the number of floors you travel, first with your support person and then alone with your partner waiting outside the elevator.

9. Travel on an elevator alone to the top of a high building without your support person.

Confronting your phobia through a series of small, incremental steps greatly reduces the difficulty of such a venture. And should your anxiety becomes undesirably high, you will learn to practice "retreat." When you retreat, you back off from a phobic situation to allow anxiety to diminish and then return to the situation minutes or perhaps an hour or two later when you feel better. In short, facing what you fear will be easier than you might think at this point. There are a number of factors built into the therapy process itself that will serve to keep your anxiety at a minimum.

The Goal of Treatment

Through practicing exposure to all of the situations in your hierarchy, you will eventually overcome your phobia. That is the goal of therapy. To overcome your phobia means two things: 1) *you stop avoiding* your phobic object or situation, and 2) *you are comfortable*, i.e., have little or no anxiety, in the presence of your phobic object or situation. For example, overcoming a fear of flying means you would be able to fly anywhere you want comfortably. Overcoming a fear of elevators means you could ride any elevator to any height comfortably, with a minimum of anxiety.

Meeting these two criteria—no longer avoiding and being comfortable—constitutes what is called a *mastery* outcome of therapy. Mastery is the highest standard of success possible in the treatment of phobias. It is possible in many cases *provided you do many repeated exposures and complete your hierarchy*. To fully master a phobia requires numerous exposures to the phobic situation and also successfully negotiating the most difficult exposures, the "top of the hierarchy." This means repeatedly facing the most difficult level of your hierarchy without the assistance of a support person. For example, to fully master a fear of flying, you would make several long-distance flights without your therapist or support person. To master a fear of driving freeways, you would do numerous exposures to driving in heavy traffic and/or for long distances on your own. The highest steps in a hierarchy often look impossible at the outset. Yet they can be handled after you have successfully negotiated all of the earlier steps. There is a rule in the treatment of phobias that is important to remember: repeated exposure will *always* overcome a phobia if you practice it long enough. You can desensitize to anything you fear if you expose yourself to it a sufficient number of times.

It may have occurred to you that in some cases full mastery of a phobia may not be a realistic goal. This might be due to either a lack of desire on your part, or to realistic limitations which you can't control. In the first instance, you may not want to progress up to the top of your hierarchy. You may be content to be able to ride an elevator to the top of the highest building in your town (perhaps twenty stories) without desiring to ride elevators to the top of eighty- or one hundred-story buildings. Perhaps you are content to be able to drive six-lane freeways and have no desire to expose yourself to eight- or ten-lane freeways that exist in certain areas. In the second instance, realistic limitations may prevent you from reaching the top of a hierarchy. You may not have the financial resources to do repeated exposures to long-distance flying. It might be impractical to do repeated exposures to your upcoming professional exam, since it is only given twice per year. (In this case, repeated exposures to a mock exam would probably be helpful.) Finally, it is simply not possible to do frequent real-life exposures in the case of a phobia of lightning and thunder if you live in a part of the country where they occur infrequently. Or if you are afraid of natural disasters such as tornadoes or earthquakes, frequent *real-life* exposure is equally impossible. In such instances, your therapist would likely assist you in exposing to video or audio simulations of such events. In a few parts of the country, three-dimensional simulations of infrequent events are possible through computer-assisted "virtual exposure." This particular technique may come to be used increasingly in the future.

Whenever it is not feasible to complete your hierarchy and/or do frequent exposures, you are most likely to achieve a certain level of success in overcoming your phobia without reaching the standard of full mastery. This is referred to as a *coping* outcome of therapy. You simply learn to cope with your phobia to a satisfactory degree, either because you don't wish to go further with exposure or because it is logistically impossible to do so. In such cases you may rely on medication, particularly tranquilizers, to help you manage your anxiety on the occasional instance when you face your phobia (for example, making a flight or receiving a shot). There is nothing wrong with achieving the ability to cope better with your phobia, even if you don't attain full mastery. In most cases coping constitutes a substantial improvement over where you were with your phobia before therapy. During your first session you and your therapist should discuss whether mastery or coping is the most realistic goal for you to aim for.

Homework

Since cognitive behavioral therapy is an educational approach, you'll be asked to practice certain skills at home between sessions. At the end of each session, your therapist will give you a homework assignment. For example, after the second week you will be asked to practice an abdominal breathing exercise for five minutes three times per day, every day. In the third session you will learn how to identify and counter negative self-talk which contributes to your phobia. Then at home you'll be asked to practice writing out negative self-statements and come up with constructive counterstatements. During later sessions you will practice facing your phobia, not only during therapy sessions but on your own, with the assistance of a support person.

As you can see, your success with this therapy program depends strongly on your willingness to do weekly homework assignments. Each week, at the beginning of the session, your therapist will review how the previous week's homework went and help you with any problems that came up. If something gets in the way of your doing the homework, you and your therapist will explore why.

What you put into this therapy program is what you'll get out of it. You are likely to overcome your phobia if you put in the time and effort to do all of the assigned homework. If, for whatever reason, you do not make the time, you will likely not get much out of the therapy. So it is important for you to evaluate your own level of motivation and commitment at the outset. The homework assignments require no more time and effort than a typical course in high school. They'll be easy to complete if you have the willingness to do so. If you feel ready to make and sustain that kind of commitment, you are ready to undertake cognitive-behavioral therapy. If you don't feel ready, it would be wise to wait and begin therapy at a later time. It is important that you discuss any concerns or feelings you have about doing homework assignments with your therapist during the first two or three sessions.

Medication

Treating specific phobia, unlike other anxiety disorders, generally does not require the use of medication. In those cases where it is difficult to negotiate the early stages of exposure, your therapist may recommend a low dose of a tranquilizer, such as Klonopin, to be used only when you practice facing your phobia. In most cases, however, medication is unnecessary and better avoided. It is necessary for you to experience *some* anxiety when confronting your fear in order to desensitize properly. Tranquilizers can interfere with desensitization by masking the experience of anxiety.

Fear Questionnaire

In regard to your phobia, choose a number from the scale below to show how much you are troubled by each problem listed, and write the number in the blank.

0	1	2	3	4	5	6	7	8
Hardly at all		Slightly troublesome		Definitely troublesome		Markedly troublesome		Very severely troublesome

_____ 1. Feeling miserable or depressed

_____ 2. Feeling irritable or angry

_____ 3. Feeling tense or panicky

_____ 4. Upsetting thoughts coming into your mind

_____ 5. Feeling you or your surroundings are strange or unreal

_____ 6. Other feelings (describe)

7. How would you rate the present state of your phobic symptoms on the scale below? Please circle one number between 0 and 8.

0	1	2	3	4	5	6	7	8
No phobias present		Slightly disturbing/ not really disturbing		Definitely disturbing/ disabling		Markedly disturbing/ disabling		Very severely disturbing/ disabling

Adapted from the "Fear Questionnaire" by I. M. Marks and A. M. Matthews, 1978.

Session 1

Initial Evaluation

You have probably already completed the first session, where your therapist asked you a number of questions about the history and background of your phobia, how you have coped with it to date and what, if any, types of help you have sought. This evaluation enabled your therapist to develop a treatment plan specifically tailored to your needs. You should have also received a brief explanation of the therapy program, similar to what was described in the previous section: "About This Treatment Program." Hopefully your therapist answered any questions you have about the treatment during the first session. If not, be sure to bring them up next time. Finally, you probably completed a short self-examination rating the intensity of your symptoms. You will repeat this procedure at the end of ten sessions in order to get a concrete idea of the effectiveness of the therapy.

The nine remaining sessions outlined in this manual contain descriptions of the various concepts and skills you will be learning to help you overcome your phobia. Please read the material for each session carefully in order to support and augment what you learn each week in therapy. If you have any questions about the concepts and skills to be learned and practiced, bring them up the following session. At the end of each session you'll find a homework assignment which matches the one you'll receive from your therapist.

Session 2

Breathing and Relaxation Techniques

The purpose of this session is for you to learn how to do abdominal breathing, progressive muscle relaxation, and to visualize a relaxing scene. Abdominal breathing is a very important technique you can use to offset any anxiety that arises when you think about or directly face your phobia. Progressive muscle relaxation is a systematic method for reducing stress and tension that can aggravate your tendency to worry about your particular phobia. Practiced regularly, it can help you to feel more relaxed all of the time. Learning to visualize a peaceful scene is an important component of systematic desensitization, which you'll learn in session 5.

Abdominal Breathing

Your breathing directly reflects the level of tension you carry in your body. Under tension, your breathing usually becomes shallow and rapid, and occurs high in the chest. When relaxed, you breathe more fully, more deeply, and from your abdomen. It's difficult to be tense and to breathe from your abdomen at the same time.

Some of the benefits of abdominal breathing include:

- Increased oxygen supply to the brain and musculature.

- Stimulation of the parasympathetic nervous system. This branch of your autonomic nervous system promotes a state of calmness and quiescence. It works in a fashion exactly opposite to the sympathetic branch of your nervous system, which stimulates a state of emotional arousal and the very physiological reactions underlying panic and anxiety.

- Greater feelings of connectedness between mind and body. Anxiety and worry tend to keep you "up in your head." A few minutes of deep abdominal breathing will help bring you down into your whole body.

- Improved concentration. If your mind is racing, it's difficult to focus your attention. Abdominal breathing will help to quiet your mind.

- Abdominal breathing by itself can trigger deep relaxation.

Abdominal breathing means breathing fully from your abdomen or from the bottom of your lungs. It is exactly the reverse of the way you breathe when you're anxious or tense, which is typically shallow and high in your chest. If you're breathing from your abdomen, you can place your hand on your stomach and see it actually *rise* each time you inhale. To practice abdominal breathing, observe the following steps:

1. Place one hand on your abdomen right beneath your rib cage, preferably while sitting or lying down.

2. Inhale slowly and deeply through your nose into the bottom of your lungs (the lowest point down in your lungs you can reach). Your chest should move only slightly, while your stomach rises, pushing your hand up.

3. When you've inhaled fully, pause for a moment and then exhale fully through your nose or your mouth. Be sure to exhale fully. As you exhale, just let yourself go and imagine your entire body going loose and limp.

4. In order to fully relax, take and release ten abdominal breaths. Try to keep your breathing *smooth* and *regular* throughout, without gulping in air or exhaling suddenly. It will help to slow down your breathing if you slowly count to four ("one, two, three, four") on the inhale and then slowly count to four again on the exhale. Use the one through four count for at least the first week of practicing abdominal breathing.

5. After you've become proficient in slowing down your breathing, you can drop the one through four count if you wish. At this point, try counting backward from twenty down to one, one count after each exhale. That is, after the first exhale count "twenty," after the next "nineteen," and so on down to zero. Remember to keep your breath slow and regular throughout, inhaling through your nose, and exhaling through your nose or mouth.

6. Continue to practice abdominal breathing for five minutes. If you start to feel light-headed at any time, stop for thirty seconds and then start up again.

7. Practice abdominal breathing for *five minutes every day, three times per day, for at least two weeks.* If possible, find regular times each day to do this so that your breathing exercise becomes a habit. With practice you can learn

in a short period of time to slow down the physiological reactions underlying anxiety.

Once you feel you've gained some mastery in the use of this technique, apply it whenever you feel anxious about facing your phobia. With continued practice, you'll be able to use abdominal breathing to reduce anxiety you have in advance of facing your fear (anticipatory anxiety) as well as anxiety that may come up when you're actually in the situation.

Progressive Muscle Relaxation

Progressive muscle relaxation is a systematic technique for achieving a deep state of relaxation. It was developed by Dr. Edmund Jacobson more than fifty years ago. Dr. Jacobson discovered that a muscle could be relaxed by first tensing it for a few seconds and then releasing it. Tensing and releasing various muscle groups throughout the body produces a deep state of relaxation, which Dr. Jacobson found capable of relieving a variety of conditions, from high blood pressure to colitis.

Progressive muscle relaxation is especially helpful for people whose anxiety is strongly associated with muscle tension. This is what often leads you to say that you are "uptight" or "tense." You may experience chronic tightness in your shoulders and neck, which can be effectively relieved by progressive muscle relaxation.

Progressive muscle relaxation can help you reduce anticipatory anxiety that comes up when you think of facing your phobia. It is also useful in practicing imagery desensitization, which you'll learn in a later session.

Progressive muscle relaxation involves tensing and relaxing sixteen different muscle groups of the body. The idea is to tense each muscle group hard (not so hard that you strain, however) for about ten seconds, and then to let go of it suddenly. You then give yourself fifteen to twenty seconds to relax, noticing how the muscle group feels when relaxed in contrast to how it felt when tensed, before going on to the next group of muscles. You might also say to yourself "I am relaxing," "Letting go," "Let the tension flow away," or any other relaxing phrase during each relaxation period between successive muscle groups. Throughout the exercise, maintain your focus on your muscles. When your attention wanders, bring it back to the particular muscle group you're working on. The guidelines below describe progressive muscle relaxation in detail:

- Make sure you are in a setting that is quiet and comfortable.

- It's preferable to practice on an empty stomach—before or one hour after a meal.

- It's preferable to be seated in a recliner or lying down, with your head supported.

- When you tense a particular muscle group, do so vigorously, without straining, for seven to ten seconds. You may want to count "one-thousand-one," "one-thousand-two," and so on, as a way of marking off seconds.

- Concentrate on what is happening. Feel the buildup of tension in each particular muscle group. It is often helpful to visualize the particular muscle group being tensed.

- When you release the muscles, do so abruptly and then relax, enjoying the sudden feeling of limpness. Allow the relaxation to develop for at least fifteen to twenty seconds before going on to the next group of muscles.

- Allow all the *other* muscles in your body to remain as relaxed as possible, while tensing a particular muscle group.

- Tense and relax each muscle group once. If a particular area feels especially tight, you can tense and relax it two or three times, waiting about twenty seconds between each cycle.

Once you are comfortably supported in a quiet place, follow the detailed instructions below:

1. To begin, take three deep abdominal breaths, inhaling and exhaling slowly through your nose each time. As you exhale, imagine that tension throughout your body is flowing away.

2. Clench your fists. Hold for seven to ten seconds and then release for fifteen to twenty seconds. *Use these same time intervals for all other muscle groups.*

3. Tighten your biceps by drawing your forearms up toward your shoulders and "making a muscle" with both arms. Hold . . . and then relax.

4. Tighten your triceps—the muscles on the undersides of your upper arms—by extending your arms out straight and locking your elbows. Hold . . . and then relax.

5. Tense the muscles in your forehead by raising your eyebrows as far as you can. Hold . . . and then relax. Imagine your forehead muscles becoming smooth and limp as they relax.

6. Tense the muscles around your eyes by clenching your eyelids tightly shut. Hold . . . and then relax. Imagine sensations of deep relaxation spreading all around the area of your eyes.

7. Tighten your jaws by opening your mouth widely so that you stretch the muscles around the hinges of your jaw. Hold . . . and then relax. Let your lips part and allow your jaw to hang loose.

8. Tighten the muscles in the back of your neck by pulling your head way back, as if you were going to touch your head to your back (be gentle with this muscle group to avoid injury). Focus only on tensing the muscles in your neck. Hold . . . and then relax. Since this area is often especially tight, it's good to do the tense-relax cycle twice.

9. Take a few deep breaths and tune in to the weight of your head sinking into whatever surface it's resting on.

10. Tighten your shoulders by raising them up as if you were going to touch your ears. Hold . . . and then relax.

11. Tighten the muscles around your shoulder blades by pushing back your shoulder blades as if you were going to touch them together. Hold the tension in your shoulder blades . . . and then relax. Since this area is often especially tense, you might repeat the tense-relax sequence twice.

12. Tighten the muscles of your chest by taking in a deep breath. Hold for up to ten seconds . . . and then release slowly. Imagine any excess tension in your chest flowing away with the exhalation.

13. Tighten your stomach muscles by sucking your stomach in. Hold . . . and then release. Imagine a wave of relaxation spreading through your abdomen.

14. Tighten your lower back muscles by arching your back. (You can omit this exercise if you have lower back pain.) Hold . . . and then relax.

15. Tighten your buttock muscles by pulling them together. Hold . . . and then relax. Imagine the muscles in your hips going loose and limp.

16. Squeeze the muscles in your thighs all the way down to your knees. You will probably have to tighten your buttocks along with your thighs, since the thigh muscles attach at the pelvis. Hold . . . and then relax. Feel your thigh muscles smoothing out and relaxing completely.

17. Tighten your calf muscles by pulling your toes toward you (flex carefully to avoid cramps). Hold . . . and then relax.

18. Tighten your feet by curling your toes downward. Hold . . . and then relax.

19. Mentally scan your body for any residual tension. If a particular area remains tense, repeat one or two tense-relax cycles for that group of muscles.

20. Now imagine a wave of relaxation gradually spreading throughout your body, starting at your head and slowly penetrating every muscle group all the way down to your toes.

The entire progressive muscle relaxation sequence should take you twenty to thirty minutes the first time. With practice you may decrease the time needed to fifteen to twenty minutes.

You might want to record the above exercises on an audio cassette to expedite your early practice sessions. Or you may wish to obtain a professionally made tape of progressive muscle relaxation. Some people always prefer to use a tape, while others have the exercises so well learned after a few weeks of practice that they prefer doing them from memory.

It's important to practice progressive muscle relaxation at least once per day. Twice per day is preferable if you feel anxious much of the time; otherwise once per day is sufficient. Try to practice at approximately the same time each day so that you can develop the habit more easily.

Remember—regular practice of progressive muscle relaxation once a day will reduce anticipatory anxiety that may arise when systematically exposing yourself to your phobic situation. Progressive muscle relaxation is also useful to help you relax before doing imagery desensitization, which you'll learn in three weeks.

Visualizing a Peaceful Scene

After completing progressive muscle relaxation, it's helpful to visualize yourself in the midst of a peaceful scene. Progressive muscle relaxation addresses particular groups of muscles; imagining yourself in a very peaceful setting can give you a global sense of relaxation that frees you from anxious thoughts. The peaceful scene can be a quiet beach, a stream in the mountains, or a calm lake. Or it can be your bedroom or a cozy fireside on a cold winter night. Don't restrict yourself to reality: you can imagine, if you want to, floating on a cloud or flying on a magic carpet. The important thing is to visualize the scene in sufficient detail so that it completely absorbs your attention. Allowing yourself to be absorbed in a peaceful scene will deepen your state of relaxation, giving you actual physiological results. Your muscular tension lessens, your heart rate slows down, your breathing deepens, your capillaries open up and warm your hands and feet, and so on. A relaxing visualization constitutes a light form of self-hypnosis.

Here are two examples of peaceful scenes.

❖

You're walking along a beautiful, deserted beach. You are barefoot and can feel the firm white sand beneath your feet as you walk along the margin of the sea. You can hear the sound of the surf as the waves ebb and flow. The sound is hypnotic, relaxing you more and more. The water is a beautiful turquoise blue flecked with whitecaps far out where the waves are cresting. Near the horizon you can see a small sailboat gliding smoothly along. The sound of the waves breaking on the shore lulls you deeper and deeper into relaxation. You draw in the fresh, salty smell of the air with each breath. Your skin glows with the warmth of the sun. You can feel a gentle breeze against your cheek and ruffling your hair. Taking in the whole scene, you feel very calm and at ease.

❖

You're snuggled in your sleeping bag. Daylight is breaking in the forest. You can feel the rays of the sun beginning to warm your face. The dawn sky stretches above you in pastel shades of pink and orange. You can smell the fresh, pine fragrance of the surrounding woods. Nearby you can hear the rushing waters of a mountain stream. The crisp, cool morning air is refreshing and invigorating. You're feeling very cozy, comfortable, and secure.

Note that these scenes are described in language that appeals to the senses of sight, hearing, touch, and smell. Using multisensory words helps to make the scene more compelling, enabling you to experience it as if you were actually there. The whole point of imagining a peaceful scene is to transport yourself from your normal state of restless thinking into an altered state of deep relaxation.

You may want to design your own peaceful scene. Be sure to describe it in vivid detail, appealing to as many senses as possible. It may help to answer the following questions: What does the scene look like? What colors are prominent? What sounds are present? What time of day is it? What is the temperature? What are you touching or in physical contact with in the scene? What does the air smell like? Are you alone or with somebody else?

Just as with progressive muscle relaxation, you may wish to record your peaceful scene on tape so that you can conjure it up without effort. You might want to record your scene on the same tape following the instructions for progressive muscle relaxation.

Use the script below to introduce your peaceful scene when you make your own recording:

❖

... Just think of relaxing every muscle in your body, from the top of your head to the tips of your toes.

... As you exhale, imagine releasing any remaining tension from your body, mind, or thoughts ... just let that stress go.

... And with every breath you inhale, feel your body drifting deeper ... down deeper into total relaxation.

... And now imagine going to your peaceful scene.... Imagine your special place as vividly as possible, as if you were really there. (Insert your peaceful scene.)

... You are very comfortable in your beautiful place, and there is no one to disturb you.... This is the most peaceful place in the world for you.... Just imagine yourself there, feeling a sense of peace flow through you and a sense of well-being. Enjoy these positive feelings.... Allow them to grow stronger and stronger.

... And remember, anytime you wish, you can return to this special place by just taking time to relax.

... These peaceful and positive feelings of relaxation can grow stronger and stronger each time you choose to relax.

Once you have imagined your own ideal peaceful scene, practice returning to it every time you do progressive muscle relaxation, deep breathing, or any other relaxation technique. This will help to reinforce the scene in your mind. After a while it will be so solidly established that you will be able to return to it on the spur of the moment—whenever you wish to calm yourself and turn off anxious thinking. This technique is one of the quickest and most effective tools you can use to counter ongoing anxiety or stress during the day.

Homework

Homework for session 2 is as follows:

1. Practice abdominal breathing for five minutes three times per day. It is best to sit or lie down while you practice.

2. Practice progressive muscle relaxation for twenty to twenty-five minutes at least once per day, having someone read the instructions or using a tape with instructions prerecorded. After several times, you may remember the sequence of exercises on your own.

3. Practice visualizing a peaceful scene after each occasion when you practice progressive muscle relaxation. Work on visualizing the scene in as much detail as possible. Use one of the preceding scenes or feel free to make up your own.

Session 3

Changing Negative Self-Talk That Contributes to Your Phobia

In this session you will learn to identify and counter unproductive self-talk that aggravates anxiety when you think about your phobia. You will use a special worksheet to write out unhelpful, scary thoughts and then counter these with more supportive, constructive ideas. After countering your negative self-talk in writing a number of times, you will begin to do it automatically.

Changing Self-Talk

Three factors tend to perpetuate fears and phobias: 1) sensitization, 2) avoidance, and 3) negative, distorted self-talk. A phobia develops when you become sensitized to a particular situation, object, or event—in other words, when anxiety becomes conditioned or associated with that situation, object, or event. If panic suddenly arises while you happen to be flying or riding an elevator, you may start feeling anxious every time you're in either of these situations. Becoming *sensitized* means that the mere presence of—or even thinking about—a situation may be enough to trigger anxiety automatically.

After sensitization occurs, you may start to *avoid* the situation. Repeated avoidance is very rewarding, because it saves you from having to feel any anxiety. Avoidance is the most powerful way to hold on to a phobia, because it prevents you from ever learning that you can handle the situation. We will deal with the sensitization and avoidance aspects of your phobia starting next week.

The third factor that perpetuates fears and phobias is distorted self-talk. The more *worry* and *anticipatory anxiety* you experience about something you fear, the more likely you are involved in unconstructive self-talk connected with that fear. You may also have negative *images* about what could happen if you had to face what you fear, or about your worst fears coming true. Both the negative self-talk and negative images serve to perpetuate your fear, guaranteeing that you remain afraid. They also undermine your confidence about ever getting over your fear. By reducing your negative self-talk and negative images, you'll be more likely to overcome your avoidance and confront your phobia.

Phobias come in many forms, but the nature of fearful self-talk is always the same. Whether you are afraid of crossing bridges, heights, or getting a shot, the types of distorted thinking which perpetuate these fears are the same. There are *two* basic distortions:

1. *Overestimating a Negative Outcome:* overestimating the odds of something bad happening. Most of the time your worries consist of "What if" statements which overestimate a particular negative outcome. For example, "What if I panic and lose complete control of myself?" "What if the plane crashes?" "What if I flunk the exam and have to drop out of school?"

2. *Underestimating Your Ability to Cope:* not recognizing or acknowledging your ability to cope with the situation, even if a negative outcome did, in fact, occur. This underestimation of your ability to cope is usually implicit in your overestimating thoughts.

If you take any fear and examine the negative thinking that contributes to maintaining that fear, you'll probably find these two distortions. To the extent that you can overcome these distortions with more reality-based thinking, the fear will tend to diminish. In essence, you can define fear as *the unreasonable overestimation of some threat, coupled with an underestimation of your ability to cope.*

Here are some examples of how the two types of distortions operate with various fears. In each example, both types of distorted thoughts are identified. Then the distortions are challenged in each case and modified with more appropriate, reality-based counterstatements.

Example 1: Fear of Driving on a Freeway

Overestimating Thoughts: "What if I can't handle the car? What if my attention wanders and I lose control of the car? What if I cause an accident and kill someone?"

Underestimating Your Ability To Cope: "I couldn't cope if I lost control of the car, especially if I got into an accident. What would I say to a policeman—that I'm phobic? I wouldn't be able to start driving again if I got stopped for a ticket. I couldn't live with myself if I caused physical injury to another person—and I know I couldn't face life myself in a wheelchair."

It's possible to refute each of these types of distorted thinking with questions and counterstatements. Examples follow:

Challenging Your Overestimating Thoughts: With overestimating thoughts, the appropriate question is: *"Viewing the situation objectively, what are the odds of the negative outcome actually happening?"*

In the case of the previous example, the question is, "If I did panic while driving, what are the actual odds that I would lose control of the car?"

Here is an example of a counterstatement you might use: "It's unlikely that having a panic attack would cause me to lose complete control of the car. The moment I felt my anxiety coming on, I could pull over to the shoulder on the side of the road and stop. If there weren't any shoulders, I could slow down in the right lane, perhaps to forty-five mph, put my flashers on, and keep a grip on myself until I reached the nearest exit. Once I got off the freeway, my panic would begin to subside."

Challenging Your Underestimation of Your Ability to Cope: Countering the idea that you couldn't cope often takes place in the process of answering overestimating thoughts with a more objective appraisal. However, the process isn't complete until you actually identify and list specific ways in which you would cope. The operative question is: *"If the worst happened, what could I do to cope?"* In the above example, some possible coping strategies might include: "If I did have a panic attack on the freeway, I would cope by getting off the highway immediately or driving slowly to the nearest exist and getting off. In the very unlikely case that I actually caused an accident, I would still cope. I would exchange names and addresses with other parties involved. If my car were undriveable, the police would likely drive me to a place where I would call to have the car towed. It would be a very unpleasant experience, to say the least; but, realistically, I would continue to function. I've functioned in emergencies in the past, and I could function in this case, if I weren't injured. Even given the unlikely possibility that I were injured, I wouldn't 'go crazy' or 'totally lose it.' I would simply wait until the paramedics came and took charge of the situation."

Example 2: Fear of Flying

Overestimating Thoughts: "With my luck, the plane might get into bad weather. What if it *did* go down?" "Even if the plane makes it, what if I get claustrophobic sitting there for two hours? What if I panic?"

Challenging: "What are the realistic odds that I'll be in a plane crash?" "What is the actual likelihood that I'll panic while aboard the plane? If I do panic, what are the realistic odds I'll feel horribly or irreparably trapped?"

Counterstatements: "The realistic odds of my plane crashing, no matter what the weather or turbulence encountered, is one in seven million." (This is actually the case.) "I'm less likely to panic during the flight if I have a support person with me or if I get up several times from my seat to walk in the aisle. The perception of being trapped is an illusion based on the fact that I have a lot of energy without the ability to release it through activity."

Underestimating Ability to Cope: (Imagining the worst) "There is no way I could cope if the plane went down. I don't see how I could cope with panicking and the feeling of being trapped. I'd lose control and freak out."

Challenging: "If the worst happened, what could I actually do?"

Coping Strategies: "Probably no one would cope very well if the plane went down. However, there would be very little time to think about it—it would all be over before I had time to react for very long. Also, I would feel no pain because I would be unconscious before I had any time to perceive physical pain. I can resist the temptation to imagine this scenario by reminding myself of the odds of being in a plane crash. I would have to fly every single day for nineteen thousand years before my 'number would be up.'

"Suppose I did panic midflight. I could use any of several anxiety management strategies to handle it—i.e., abdominal breathing, walking up and down the aisle, coping statements, talking to my support person (or calling someone on a cellular phone, if available). I could even take medication, if necessary. I'm confident that *something* would help me to feel better after a few minutes."

Example 3: Fear of Contracting a Serious Illness

Overestimating Thoughts: "I have no energy and feel tired all the time. Maybe I'm developing cancer and don't know it!"

Challenging: "What are the odds that symptoms of low energy and fatigue mean that I'm developing cancer?"

Counterstatements: "Symptoms of fatigue and low energy can be indicative of all kinds of physical and psychological conditions, including a low-grade virus, anemia, adrenal exhaustion or hypothyroidism, depression, and food allergies, to name a few. There are many possible explanations of my condition, and I don't have any specific symptoms that would indicate cancer. So the odds of my fatigue and low energy indicating cancer are very low."

Underestimating Ability to Cope: "If I were diagnosed with cancer, that would be the end. I couldn't take it. I'd be better off ending things quickly and killing myself."

Challenging: "If the unlikely happened and I really were diagnosed with cancer, what could I actually do about it?"

Coping Strategies: "As bad as a cancer diagnosis would be, it's unlikely that I would totally go to pieces. After an initial difficult adjustment to the fact—which might takes days to weeks—I would most likely begin to think about what I needed to do to deal with the situation. It would certainly be difficult, yet it wouldn't be a situation that I was less equipped to handle than anyone else. My doctor and I would plan the most effective possible treatment strategies. I would join a local cancer support group and get lots of support from my friends and immediate family. I would try alternative methods, such as visualization and dietary changes, which could help. In short, I would try everything possible to attempt to heal the condition."

Restructuring Unhelpful Self-Talk

The above three examples illustrate how overestimating thoughts can be challenged and then countered by more realistic, less anxiety-provoking thinking. During the next week, monitor the times when you feel anxious or panicky. Each time you do, use the following five steps to work with negative self-talk.

1. If you're feeling anxious or upset, do something to relax, such as abdominal breathing, progressive muscle relaxation, or meditation. It's easier to notice your internal dialogue when you take time to slow down and relax.

2. After you get somewhat relaxed, ask yourself, "What was I telling myself that made me anxious?" or "What was going through my mind?" Make an effort to separate thoughts from feelings. For example, "I felt terrified" describes a feeling, while "I will lose control of myself" is an overestimating thought that might lead you to feel terrified. Sometimes feelings and thoughts occur together in one statement: "I'm scared I will lose control." The negative thought here is still "I will lose control."

3. Identify the two basic types of distortions within your anxious self-talk. Sort out *overestimating thoughts*, and *thoughts that underestimate your ability to cope*. Note that overestimating thoughts frequently begin with "What if . . . ." Thoughts that underestimate your ability to cope might begin with "I can't . . ." or "I won't be able . . ."

4. When you've identified your anxious, distorted thoughts, *challenge* them with appropriate questions.

   For overestimating thoughts: "What are the realistic odds that this feared outcome will actually happen? Has this outcome ever happened to me before?"

   For thoughts underestimating your ability to cope: "What coping skills can I bring to bear to handle anxiety? If the worst outcome I fear *does* occur, what could I actually *do* to cope?"

5. Write counterstatements to each of your overestimating thoughts. These counterstatements should contain language and logic that reflect more balanced, realistic thinking. Then make a list of ways you might cope with your phobic situation, including what you would do if your most feared outcome actually occurred.

Use the Worry Worksheet (also known as Self-Talk Worksheet) to write down your anxious thoughts and corresponding counterstatements for your specific fear or phobia. In the section at the bottom, list ways in which you would cope if the negative (but unlikely) outcome you fear actually occurred.

The Worry Worksheet

Specific Fear or Phobia _____

Anxious Self-Talk	Counterstatements
Overestimating thoughts (or images): "What if . . ."	

Coping Strategies: First, list ways in which you can cope with your phobic situation. Second, list ways in which you would cope if a negative (but unlikely) outcome did occur. Use the other side of the sheet if needed. Change "What if" to *What I would do if (one of your negative predictions actually did come about) . . ."*

1.

2.

3.

Make twenty copies of this worksheet before you start, and use a separate sheet each time you practice disputing your negative self-talk.

Homework

Homework for session 3 is as follows:

1. Make twenty copies of the Worry Worksheet and use it each day to work with anticipatory anxiety that comes up around facing your phobic situation. Write down overestimating "What if . . ." thoughts that keep your fear going, and refute each one with a more reasonable, self-supporting counterstatement. Then write down coping strategies, including both: 1) how you see yourself coping when you actually begin to confront your phobia, and 2) how you would cope if your worst fear about the situation came true. Bring in your worksheets to therapy the following week.

2. Continue practicing abdominal breathing and progressive muscle relaxation daily, as in the homework for session 2.

Session 4

Anxiety Coping Strategies

The purpose of this session is to learn and practice useful strategies you can use to diminish anxiety that may arise when you actually face your fear later in the therapy. These strategies consist of: 1) abdominal breathing (which you've already learned), 2) using a special anxiety scale to monitor your level of anxiety, 3) repeating positive coping statements in advance of as well as when you directly confront your phobic situation, and 4) using other diversion techniques such as talking to your support person, moving about, or focusing on your immediate surroundings. Practicing these techniques now will help to make them more readily available to you when you begin to face your fear in real life. In this session you will also learn some "worry management" techniques to help reduce your tendency to worry be-fore you confront your phobia.

The Anxiety Scale

With practice you can learn to identify the preliminary signs that anxiety is beginning to develop. For some persons this might be a sudden quickening of heartbeat. For others it might be a tightening in the chest, sweaty hands, or queasiness. Still others might experience a slight dizziness or disorientation. Most people experience some preliminary warning symptoms before reaching the "point of no return" where a panic attack is inevitable.

It's possible to distinguish among different levels or degrees of anxiety by imagining a ten-point scale.

Anxiety Scale

7–10: *Major Panic Attack*	All of the symptoms in level 6 exaggerated; terror; fear of going crazy or dying; compulsion to escape
6: *Moderate Panic Attack*	Palpitations; difficulty breathing; feeling disoriented or detached (feeling of unreality); panic in response to perceived loss of control
5: *Early Panic*	Heart pounding or beating irregularly; constricted breathing; spaciness or dizziness; definite fear of losing control; compulsion to escape
4: *Marked Anxiety*	Feeling uncomfortable or "spacey"; heart beating fast; muscles tight; *beginning to question your ability to maintain control*
3: *Moderate Anxiety*	Feeling uncomfortable but still in control; heart starting to beat faster; more rapid breathing; muscles tightening; sweaty palms
2: *Mild Anxiety*	Butterflies in stomach; muscle tension; definitely nervous
1: *Slight Anxiety*	Passing twinge of anxiety, feeling slightly nervous
0: *Relaxation*	Calm, a feeling of being undistracted and at peace

The symptoms at various levels of this scale are typical, although they may not correspond exactly to your own symptoms. The important thing is to identify what constitutes a level 4 for *you*. This is the point at which—whatever symptoms you're experiencing—*you feel your control over your reaction beginning to diminish.* Up to and through level 3, you may be feeling anxious and uncomfortable, but you still feel that you're coping. Starting at level 4, you begin to wonder whether you can manage what's happening, which can lead you to escalate your anxiety further. With practice you can learn to "catch yourself" and limit your reaction *before* it reaches the point of no return. The more adept you become at recognizing slight to moderate levels of anxiety up through level 4 on the scale, the more control you will gain over your anxiety.

Abdominal Breathing

Abdominal breathing is the most important skill you can use to manage anxiety that comes up when facing a fearful situation. Three or four minutes of steady abdominal breathing will generally diminish mild to moderate levels of anxiety (levels 2 and 3 on the Anxiety Scale) and can usually interrupt the upward momentum of anxiety at level 4. Even if anxiety reaches a panic level, abdominal breathing can help to reduce it.

As a general rule, it's good to practice abdominal breathing just before you begin to confront your phobia and continue it the whole time you are in the situation.

Focusing on your breathing will help to keep you more grounded, in the present, and less prone to focus on unconstructive thoughts.

Coping Statements

It's often helpful when confronting a phobia to work with coping statements. These are positive statements you can say to yourself just before you begin to face your phobic situation—or to help manage anxiety during the exposure process itself.

The purpose of using coping statements is to help divert your mind from any negative, anxiety-provoking self-talk you might be prone to engage in when you face what you fear. These positive statements also help put your mind in a positive frame. They can help you relax and maintain your confidence just before or during the time you confront your phobia. Any anxiety you experience during exposure to your phobia tends to make you more suggestible. By repeating positive coping statements at the time of exposure, you can suggest a positive state of mind that can help minimize anxiety.

There are two ways in which you might want to work with coping statements. First, you might want to record your favorite statements on an audio cassette and listen to them several times before you directly confront your phobic situation. If you have a portable cassette recorder with headphones, you might even want to listen to them during the exposure process itself.

An alternative, more active way to work with coping statements is to write them down on three-by-five file cards—one or two statements per card. Keep the cards in your purse or wallet and then take them out and rehearse the coping statements before or during your exposure sessions. Some people find repeating a single coping statement over and over to be more effective, while others like to read down a list of several coping statements.

Keep in mind that to get the most benefit from coping statements, you will need to practice working with them many times. They may not be as effective in offsetting anxiety the first few times you use them as they will be after repeated practice. It took many repetitions to reinforce your negative, anxiety-provoking self-statements that trigger your anxiety. By the same token, it will take repeated use of positive coping statements—before or during real-life exposure—to reach a point where you fully internalize them.

The following coping statements are divided into three categories: statements to use when you are *preparing* to face your phobic situation; statements you can use when you *first confront* the situation and *during* the exposure process; and, finally, statements you can use to help you handle any symptoms or feelings that come up during exposure.

Preparing to Face Your Phobia

- Today I'm willing to go just a little outside my comfort zone.

- This is an opportunity for me to learn to become comfortable with this situation.

- Facing my fear of _____ is the best way to overcome my anxiety about it.

- Each time I choose to face _____, I take another step toward becoming free of fear.

- By taking this step now, I'll eventually be able to do what I want.

- There's no right way to do this. Whatever happens is fine.

- I know I'll feel better once I'm actually in the situation.

- Whatever I do, I'll do the best I can.

- I praise myself for being willing to confront my fear of _____.

- There's always a way to retreat from this situation if I need to.

First Confronting (and During Exposure to) Your Phobia

- I've handled this before and I can handle it now.

- Relax and go slowly. There's no need to push right now.

- I can take some abdominal breaths and take my time.

- Nothing serious is going to happen to me.

- It's okay to take my time with this and do only as much as I'm ready to do today.

- I'm going to be all right. I've succeeded with this before.

- I don't have to do this perfectly. I can let myself be human.

- I can think about being in my peaceful place as I undertake this.

- I can monitor my anxiety level and retreat from this situation if I need to.

- This is not as bad as I thought.

- As I continue to practice exposure, it will get easier.

- If I'm feeling anxiety, I'm already in the process of desensitizing.

Coping With Body Sensations and Feelings That Come Up During Exposure

- I can handle these symptoms or sensations.

- These feelings are just a reminder to use my coping skills.

- I can take some abdominal breaths and allow these feelings to pass.

- These feelings will pass and I'll be okay.

- This is just adrenaline—it will pass in a few minutes.

- This will pass soon.

- These are just thoughts—not reality.

- This is just anxiety—I'm not going to let it get to me.

- Nothing about these sensations or feelings is dangerous.

- I don't need to let these feelings and sensations stop me. I can continue to function.

- It's always okay to retreat for a while if I need to.

- This feeling isn't comfortable or pleasant, but I can accept it.

- I'll just let my body do its thing. This will pass.

- I can take all the time I need in order to let go and relax.

- There's no need to push myself. I can take as small a step forward as I choose.

- This anxiety won't hurt me—even if it doesn't feel good.

- I don't need these thoughts—I can choose to think differently.

Other Diversion Techniques

Any technique that helps you to redirect your attention away from anxiety symptoms and fear-provoking thoughts can be helpful when you're confronting your phobic situation. While abdominal breathing and coping statements should be your first line of defense, any of the following strategies can be useful, especially at levels of anxiety up to and including level 4 in the Anxiety Scale.

- Talk to another person (this could be your support person or someone you call on a cellular phone).

- Move around or engage in physical activity.

- Engage in a simple, repetitive activity (count from 100 backwards during a long elevator ride, for example).

- Express angry feelings (get angry at the phobia—but do *not* vent anger on people).

- Anchor yourself in your immediate environment. Focus on concrete objects in your surroundings, even touch them if that helps.

- Practice thought stopping. Shout the word "Stop" once or twice—or snap a rubber band against your wrist. This will help disrupt a chain of negative thoughts. Follow this with abdominal breathing or by repeating a positive affirmation.

Putting It All Together: Integrated Anxiety Management

In general, should anxiety symptoms come on during exposure, use the following three-step technique to manage them.

Accept the symptoms. Don't fight or resist them. Resisting or fleeing symptoms of anxiety tends to make them worse. The more you can adopt an attitude of acceptance, no matter how unpleasant the symptoms may be, the better your ability to cope. *Acceptance prepares you to do something proactive about your anxiety rather than getting caught up in reactions to it.*

Breathe. Practice abdominal breathing. When anxiety first comes up, always go to abdominal breathing. If you have been practicing abdominal breathing regularly, merely initiating it provides a cue to your body to relax and disengage from a potential "fight or flight" response.

Cope. Use a coping strategy. After you begin to feel centered in abdominal breathing, use a coping statement or a diversion technique (for example, talking to your support person) to continue to manage your feelings during exposure. *Any coping technique will reinforce the basic stance of not giving attention or energy to negative thoughts and/or uncomfortable body sensations. By regularly practicing coping techniques, you reinforce an attitude of efficacy and mastery—instead of passive submission and victimization—in the face of your anxiety.* Be aware that abdominal breathing is itself a coping strategy, and sometimes it alone will be enough.

What To Do If Anxiety Exceeds Level 4

If you are unable to arrest an anxiety reaction before it goes beyond your personal "point of no return," observe the following guidelines:

- Leave the situation if possible. Try to return to it later the same day if you can.

- Don't try to control or fight your symptoms—accept them and "ride them out"; remind yourself that your reaction is not dangerous and will pass.

- Talk to someone, if available. Express your feelings to them (if in a car or aboard a plane alone, you might use a cellular phone).

- Move around or engage in physical activity.

- Focus on simple objects around you.

- Touch the floor, the physical objects around you, or "ground" yourself in some other way.

- Breathe slowly and regularly through your nose to reduce possible symptoms of hyperventilation.

- As a last resort, take an extra dose of a minor tranquilizer (with the approval of your doctor).

If you have a panic attack, you may feel temporarily very confused and disorientated. Try asking yourself the following questions to increase your objectivity (you may want to write these out on a three-by-five card which you carry with you during exposure).

1. *Are these symptoms I'm feeling truly dangerous?* (Answer: No)

2. *What is the absolute worst thing that could happen?* (Usual answer: I might have to leave this situation quickly or I might have to ask for assistance.)

3. *Am I telling myself anything that is making this worse?*

4. *What is the most supportive thing I could do for myself right now?*

Worry Management Strategies

Ultimately the best treatment for anticipatory anxiety—worry in advance of facing a phobia—is exposure. Anticipatory anxiety may not clear up entirely until you have mastered your phobic situation. You can count on being relatively free of worry about your phobia when you've desensitized to it and no longer have the need to avoid it.

Prior to undertaking exposure, you are likely to have some worry about facing your fear, if you don't worry about it already. Worry is like a negative spiral. The longer you spend time with it, the deeper into it you can get. It may also be viewed as a form of trance. The more you induce it by repetition, the more entranced you may become, and the more difficult it is to "break the spell."

It takes a deliberate act of will to stop worry. You need to make a deliberate effort to move away from circular mental activity in your mind by "shifting gears" to another modality of experience, such as bodily activity, expressing emotions, interpersonal communication, sensory distraction, or a specific ritual. Although deliberately choosing to break out of an obsessive worry may be difficult at first (especially if you're highly anxious), with practice it will get easier.

Here are a few strategies that will help you to move away from worry.

Do physical exercise. This can be your favorite outdoor or indoor exercise, dancing, or just household chores. Focus on your body while doing the exercise.

Do progressive muscle relaxation alone or in combination with abdominal breathing. Keep this up for five to twenty minutes until you feel relaxed and free of worry-thoughts.

Take action on the issue that causes you worry. If you're afraid of flying, read a book or listen to tape on overcoming that fear (your therapist can recommend one). If you're afraid of getting a shot, practice your imagery desensitization. If you're afraid of contracting cancer, devote energy to health practices such as exercise and good nutrition.

Talk to someone. Converse (in person or on the phone) about something other than the worry, unless you want to express your feelings about it.

Confront your worry on paper. Write out on a piece of paper the negative "What if" statements that make up your worry. Then take another sheet and write constructive counterstatements to each of your What if statements (use the Worry Worksheet from the previous week, if you wish).

Use visual distractions. This can be TV, movies, video games, your computer, uplifting reading, or even a rock garden.

Use sensory-motor distraction. Try arts and crafts, repairing something, gardening.

Practice healthy rituals. Combine abdominal breathing with a positive affirmation that has personal significance. Keep this up for five to ten minutes, or until you're fully relaxed. (This is actually a positive trance induction to overcome the negative trance enforced by the obsessive worry.)

Examples of affirmations:	*(for the spiritually inclined)*
• "Let it go."	• "Let go and let God."
• "These are just thoughts—they're fading away."	• "I Abide in Spirit (God)."
• "I'm whole, relaxed, and free of worry."	• "I release this negativity to God."

Use thought stopping. Say the word "Stop!" emphatically several times. If you prefer, snap a rubber band against your wrist or throw a wet washrag over your face. Following this, use any of the preceding techniques. Thought stopping alone will probably only temporarily disrupt a worry pattern, but it is a good way to initially break that pattern.

Remember that you can stop worrying by using any or all of these strategies. *It is necessary, however, to practice.* The more you utilize these techniques, the more mastery you will achieve in overcoming useless worry.

Homework

Homework for this week is as follows:

1. Practice anxiety-management techniques, including abdominal breathing, coping statements, and diversion techniques at any time when you feel anxiety symptoms beginning to come on during the week. After you have become proficient at using several different techniques, try combining coping statements or diversion techniques with abdominal breathing. Remember the three-step approach: 1) *accept* anxiety symptoms, 2) *breathe* slowly from your abdomen to reduce them, and then 3) *cope*, applying coping statements or other diversion techniques until you feel better. Keep in

mind that sometimes abdominal breathing alone for a few minutes will be all you need to do.

2. Use worry reduction techniques to directly offset your tendency to worry should it arise during the week. Pick two or three preferred techniques from the list and practice them regularly.

3. Continue challenging and restructuring negative self-talk associated with your phobia using the Worry Worksheet.

4. Continue practicing abdominal breathing and progressive muscle relaxation on a regular basis.

Imagery Desensitization

This session focuses on learning to face your phobia in imagery. Visualizing yourself in your particular phobic situation will help you to habituate or "desensitize" both to the stimuli associated with that situation as well as to your own internal thoughts and fantasies about the situation. You will practice imagery desensitization for two weeks before undertaking real-life exposure to your phobia. Spending time now doing imagery work will help make real-life exposure easier later. In some cases imagery desensitization (along with audio and video simulations of your phobic situation) is the *only* exposure method that is practical or possible.

The "Cure" for Any Phobia Is to Face It

The most effective way to overcome a phobia is simply to face it. Continuing to avoid a situation that frightens you is, more than anything else, what keeps the phobia alive.

Having to face a particular situation you have been avoiding for years may at the outset seem an impossible task. Yet this task can be made manageable by breaking it down into a number of small steps. Instead of entering a situation all at once, you can do it very gradually in small or even minute increments. And instead of confronting the situation directly in real life, you can face it first in your imagination. This is where imagery desensitization comes in.

Sensitization and Desensitization

Sensitization is a process of becoming sensitized to a particular stimulus. In the case of phobias, it involves learning to associate anxiety with a particular situation. Perhaps you once panicked or experienced high anxiety while confronting your phobic situation. If your anxiety level was high enough, it's likely that you acquired a strong association between being in that particular situation and being anxious. Thereafter, being in, near, or perhaps just thinking about the situation automatically triggered your anxiety: a connection between the situation and a strong anxiety response was established. Because this connection was automatic and seemingly beyond your control, you probably did all you could to avoid putting yourself in the situation again. Your avoidance was rewarded because it saved you from reexperiencing your anxiety. At the point where you began to *always* avoid the situation, you developed a full-fledged phobia.

Desensitization is the process of *unlearning* the connection between anxiety and a particular situation. For desensitization to occur, you need to enter your phobic situation while you're in a relaxed state. With *imagery desensitization*, you *visualize* being in a phobic situation while you're relaxed. If you begin to feel anxious, you retreat from your imagined phobic situation and imagine yourself instead in a very peaceful scene. With *real-life desensitization*, you confront a phobic situation directly but physically retreat to a safe place if your anxiety reaches a certain level—then return to the situation. In both cases the point is to 1) *unlearn* the connection between a phobic situation (such as getting a shot or riding an elevator) and an anxiety response, and 2) *reassociate* feelings of relaxation and calmness with that particular situation. Repeatedly visualizing a phobic situation while relaxed—or actually entering it while relaxed—will eventually allow you to overcome your tendency to respond with anxiety. If you can train yourself to relax in response to something, you will no longer feel anxious about it. Relaxation and anxiety are incompatible responses, so the goal of desensitization is to learn to remain in the phobic situation and be relaxed at the same time.

You may wonder why it's necessary to go through the desensitization process initially in your imagination. Why not just face the dreaded object or situation in real life? More than thirty years ago, the behavioral psychologist Joseph Wolpe discovered the efficacy of desensitization through imagery. In some cases it is so effective that it supplants the need for real-life desensitization. In other cases, imagery desensitization reduces anxiety sufficiently to make the task of real-life desensitization easier.

Practicing imagery desensitization before confronting a phobia in real life can also help you overcome your *anticipatory anxiety*. As you learned in the previous session, this is the anxiety you experience in anticipation of having to deal with a phobic situation. Hours or days before riding an elevator or your next plane flight, for example, you may experience numerous anxious thoughts and images about the upcoming situation. Dwelling on these anxious thoughts and images only creates more anxiety, long before you ever deal with the actual situation. By systematically training yourself to relax as you imagine scenes of a future phobic situation, you can reduce your anticipatory anxiety substantially.

Success with imagery desensitization depends on four things:

1. Your capacity to attain a deep state of relaxation.

2. Constructing an appropriate *hierarchy*: a series of scenes or situations relating to your phobia which are ranked from mildly anxiety-provoking to very anxiety-provoking.

3. The vividness and detail with which you can visualize each scene in the hierarchy.

4. Your patience and perseverance in practicing desensitization on a regular basis.

A hierarchy is helpful because each new step is only slightly more anxiety-provoking than the one before, so you can progress very gradually toward a full confrontation with your fear.

Constructing an Appropriate Hierarchy

A well-constructed hierarchy allows you to approach a phobic situation gradually through a sequence of steps. The following steps are involved:

1. Select the phobic situation you want to work on.

2. Imagine having to deal with this situation in a very limited way—one that hardly bothers you at all. You can create this scenario by imagining yourself somewhat removed in space or time from full exposure to the situation—such as merely walking up to an elevator without going in, or imagining your feelings one month before you are going to make a flight. Or you can diminish the difficulty of the situation by visualizing yourself with a supportive person at your side. Try in these ways to create a very mild scenario of facing your phobia and designate it as the first step in your hierarchy.

3. Now imagine what would be the strongest or most challenging scene relating to your phobia, and place it at the opposite extreme as the highest step in your hierarchy. For example, if you're phobic about supermarkets, your highest step might be waiting in a long busy at the checkout counter by yourself. For flying, such a step might involve taking off on a transcontinental flight or encountering severe air turbulence midflight.

4. Now develop six to eight scenes of varying intensity between your mildest and most challenging scene. Place these scenes in ascending order between the two extremes you've already defined. See if you can identify what specific parameters of your phobia make you more or less anxious and use them to develop scenes of varying intensity.

There are four different variables you might consider in developing imagery scenes of varying intensity:

Spatial proximity. How close you are physically to the feared object or situation. In the case of flying, for example, you would likely feel more anxiety watching planes land and take off than you would merely seeing the airport terminal. Or seeing a picture of a jet might be less anxiety-provoking than standing next to one in real life.

Temporal proximity. How close you are in time to the feared object or situation. For example, you might be likely to feel more anxiety one hour before receiving a shot or taking an exam than the night before or three days before.

Length or duration of exposure. This refers to how long you are in a situation. Ten minutes in a shopping mall is likely to be more difficult than two minutes.

Intensity of exposure. Intensity of exposure is often closely related to duration. Riding up twenty floors in an elevator is a stronger, more intense exposure than riding up five floors. Having a blood sample taken is usually a more intense exposure than getting a shot, which is in turn more intense than watching someone else receive a shot.

Degree of support. How close you are to a support person during exposure. In driving on a freeway, you might imagine your support person sitting next to you, following you in a second car, following you a half mile back, or simply waiting for you at your destination.

Your hierarchy may vary in terms of just one of these variables or perhaps three or four. For example, the following hierarchy relating to driving on freeways varies in terms of three distinct parameters: 1) duration (or distance) driven, 2) degree of support, 3) degree of traffic congestion (one aspect of intensity).

Phobia About Driving on Freeways

1. Watching from a distance as cars drive past on the freeway

2. Riding in a car on the freeway with someone else driving (this could be broken down into several steps, varying the distance traveled or time spent on the freeway)

3. Driving on the freeway the distance of one exit with a support person sitting next to you at a time when there is little traffic

4. Driving the distance of one exit with a support person when the freeway is busier (but not at rush hour)

5. Repeat step 3 alone

6. Repeat step 4 alone

7. Driving the distance of two or three exits with a support person sitting next to you at a time when there is little traffic

8. Driving the distance of two or three exits with a support person sitting next to you at a time when there is moderate traffic

9. Repeat step 7 alone

10. Repeat step 8 alone

In steps above this level you would increase the distance you drive and also include driving under rush hour conditions.

In the next example (involving getting a shot) the hierarchy varies in terms of spatial proximity and intensity of exposure.

Phobia About Getting Injections

1. Watching a movie in which a minor character gets a shot
2. A friend talking about her flu shot
3. Making a routine doctor's appointment
4. Driving to a medical center
5. Parking your car in the medical center parking lot
6. Thinking about shots in the doctor's waiting room
7. A woman coming out of the treatment room rubbing her arm
8. A nurse with a tray of syringes walking past
9. Entering an examination room
10. A doctor entering the room and asking you about your symptoms
11. The doctor saying you need an injection
12. A nurse entering the room with injection materials
13. The nurse filling a syringe
14. The smell of alcohol being applied to a cotton ball
15. A hypodermic needle poised in the doctor's hand
16. Receiving a penicillin shot in the buttocks
17. Receiving a flu shot in the arm
18. Having a large blood sample taken

Note that in both examples, increments from one step to the next are very small. One of the keys to success with imagery desensitization is to create a hierarchy with small enough steps so that it is relatively easy to progress from one to the next.

Generally, eight to twelve steps in a hierarchy are sufficient, although in some cases you may want to include as many as twenty. Fewer than eight steps is usually an insufficient number to make the hierarchy meaningful.

Procedure for Imagery Desensitization

Desensitization through imagery is a two-step process. First, you need to take the time to get very relaxed. Second, you go through the desensitization process itself, which involves alternating back and forth between visualizing a particular scene in your hierarchy and recapturing a feeling of deep relaxation. Be sure to follow all of the steps outlined below:

1. *Relax.* Spend ten to fifteen minutes getting relaxed. Use progressive muscle relaxation or any other relaxation technique that works well for you.

2. *Visualize yourself in your peaceful scene.* This is the relaxing place you have been visualizing when you practice relaxation.

3. *Visualize yourself in the first scene of your phobia hierarchy.* Stay there for one minute, trying to picture everything with as much vividness and detail as possible, as if you were "right there." Do *not* picture yourself as being anxious. If you see yourself in the scene at all, imagine yourself acting and feeling calm and confident—dealing with the situation in the way you would most like to. If you feel little or no anxiety (below level 2 on the Anxiety Scale), proceed to the next scene up in your hierarchy.

4. *If you experience mild to moderate anxiety (level 2 or 3 on the Anxiety Scale), spend one minute in the scene, allowing yourself to relax to it.* You can do this by breathing away any anxious sensations in your body or by repeating coping statements from the list you received last week, such as "I am calm and at ease," or "Let go and relax." *Picture yourself handling the situation in a calm and confident manner.*

5. *After one minute of exposure to the scene, retreat from the phobic scene to your peaceful scene.* Spend about one minute in your peaceful scene or long enough to get fully relaxed. Then repeat your visualization of the same phobic scene as in step 4 for one minute. Keep alternating between a given phobic scene and your peaceful scene (about one minute each) until the phobic scene loses its capacity to elicit any (or more than very mild) anxiety. Remember to use abdominal breathing and coping statements to diminish any anxiety you feel. Then you are ready to proceed to the next step up in your hierarchy.

6. *If visualizing a particular scene causes you marked anxiety (level 4 or above on the Anxiety Scale), do not spend more than ten seconds there.* Retreat immediately to your peaceful scene and stay there until you're fully relaxed. If you have difficulty relaxing in your peaceful scene, do progressive muscle relaxation for five to ten minutes until you get relaxed. Expose yourself gradually to the more difficult scenes, alternating short intervals of exposure with retreat to your peaceful scene. If a particular scene in your hierarchy continues to cause difficulty, you probably need to add another step—one that is intermediate in difficulty between the last step you completed successfully and the one that is troublesome.

7. *Continue progressing up your hierarchy step by step in imagination.* Generally it will take a minimum of two exposures to an anxiety-provoking scene to reduce your anxiety to it. An exception might be when you're desensitizing to the first few scenes in your hierarchy. Keep in mind that it's important not to proceed to a more advanced step until you're fully comfortable with the preceding step. Practice imagery desensitization for fifteen to twenty

minutes each day and begin your practice *not* with a new step but with the last step you successfully negotiated (then proceed to a new step).

To sum up, imagery desensitization involves four steps that you apply to *each* scene in your hierarchy:

1. *Visualize* the phobic scene as vividly and in as much detail as possible.

2. *React to the scene* allowing yourself to stay with it for one minute if your anxiety stays below level 4—marked anxiety. Picture yourself handling the scene in a calm and confident manner. Use abdominal breathing and coping statements to assist you in relaxing to the scene. If your anxiety to the scene reaches level 4 or above, retreat to your peaceful scene after five to ten seconds of exposure. If you still feel anxious in your peaceful scene, do ten to fifteen minutes of progressive muscle relaxation until you feel relaxed.

3. *Relax* in your peaceful scene (between exposures to phobic scenes) for up to a minute, until you're fully calm.

4. *Repeat* the process of alternating between a phobic scene and your peaceful scene until the phobic scene loses its power to elicit anxiety. At this point proceed to the next scene up in your hierarchy.

Getting the Most Out of Imagery Desensitization

The process of desensitization will work best if you adhere to the following guidelines:

❖

Spend about fifteen to twenty minutes the first time you practice imagery desensitization. As you gain skill in relaxation and visualization, you can lengthen your sessions to thirty minutes. In this time period (on a good day), you can expect to master two or three scenes in your hierarchy.

❖

You need to be very relaxed for imagery desensitization to be effective. If you feel that you aren't deeply relaxed, then you might spend more time—twenty to thirty minutes—relaxing at the outset, and also spend more time relaxing in your peaceful scene after each exposure to a particular phobic scene. Make sure that you *fully* recover from any anxiety after each exposure.

❖

You need to be able to visualize each phobic scene as well as your peaceful scene in detail, as if you were actually there. If you have difficulty with visualizing effectively, you might ask yourself the following questions about each scene to heighten its vividness and detail:

- What objects or people are in the scene?

- What colors do you see in the scene?

- Is the light bright or dim?

- What sounds can you hear in the scene?

- Can you hear the wind or a breeze?

- What is the temperature of the air?

- What are you wearing?

- Can you smell or taste anything?

- What other physical sensations are you aware of?

- What are your emotions within the scene?

❖

Stop a particular session if you feel tired, bored, or overly upset.

❖

Try to practice every day if possible. Your general anxiety level may vary from day to day, so practicing every day for two weeks will give you the opportunity to desensitize under various conditions.

❖

Even if the first few scenes in your hierarchy don't elicit any anxiety at all, it's important to expose yourself to each of them at least once. (You can proceed from one to the next without retreating to your peaceful scene if your anxiety stays below Level 2.) Imagery desensitization is at work even when you're not feeling any anxiety in response to a given scene because you are still associating relaxation with your phobia.

❖

Keep practicing until you have completed all of the scenes in your hierarchy.

Putting Imagery Desensitization on Tape

You might find it helpful to put instructions for desensitization on tape to reduce any distractions while going through the process. Use the guidelines below for making your own tape.

- Begin your tape with ten to fifteen minutes of instructions for deep relaxation. Use the instructions for progressive muscle relaxation or any visualization that can induce a state of deep relaxation.

- Following the relaxation phase, visualize yourself in your peaceful scene. Spend at least one minute there.

- After going to your peaceful scene, record your own instructions for desensitization, according to the guidelines below:

  Picture yourself in the first scene of your phobia hierarchy . . . Imagine what it would be like if you were actually there.

  (Pause fifteen to twenty seconds.)

  Now allow yourself to relax in this scene . . . do whatever you need to do to relax.

  (Pause fifteen to twenty seconds.)

  Picture yourself handling the situation in just the way you would like . . . Imagine that you are feeling relaxed, calm, and confident. You might wish to practice slow, abdominal breathing . . . and as you exhale, let out any tense or uncomfortable feelings. Also use your coping statements to relax if you wish.

  (Pause fifteen to twenty seconds.)

  Now let go of this scene and go back to your peaceful scene. Remain there until you feel fully relaxed. Put your recorder on pause if you need to until all of your anxiety is gone.

  (Let one minute elapse on the tape, then continue.)

  If you felt any anxiety imagining the previous scene in your hierarchy, go back and imagine yourself there again. . . . Take one minute to let go and relax in the context of that scene, and then return to your peaceful scene until you are fully relaxed. . . . You can place your cassette player on pause while you do this. . . . If you felt little or no anxiety within the previous scene, you're ready to go on.

  (Leave a ten-second pause on the tape, then continue.)

  Now, if you were fully relaxed in the previous scene, go on to the next scene in your hierarchy. . . . Imagine what it would be like if you were actually there.

  (Pause fifteen to twenty seconds.)

  (Repeat the above instructions a second time, starting from the phrase: "Now allow yourself to relax in this scene . . .")

Your tape should consist of 1) ten to fifteen minutes of instructions for deep relaxation, 2) instructions for going to your peaceful scene, with a minute of silence for being there, and 3) the above instructions for systematic desensitization repeated twice.

(Audio tapes by the author containing imagery desensitization protocols are available for the following phobias: fear of flying, heights, driving freeways, driving far from home, shopping in a supermarket, fear of contracting illness, giving a talk, and speaking up in public. For further information, contact New Harbinger Publications at (800) 748-6273.)

Homework

1. Practice imagery desensitization for your phobia three to five times during the week. Spend up to thirty minutes each time. Work up the steps of your hierarchy following the procedure you received. You may wish to put instructions for imagery desensitization on tape.

   Please note: If you're having difficulty reducing your anxiety with imagery desensitization, the problem may lie in one of four areas. You may need to:

   - Be more completely relaxed before you begin—desensitization works best when you're very relaxed.

   - Work on visualizing your phobic scenes, or your peaceful scene, in more detail.

   - Become completely desensitized to a particular step in your hierarchy before proceeding to the next step, or

   - Add additional steps in your hierarchy, especially if the gap" between one scene and the next one up is too wide.

2. Practice anxiety and worry management skills from session 4 as needed.

3. Continue practicing abdominal breathing and progressive muscle relaxation daily.

Session 6

Exposure Therapy

In this session you will learn about *exposure*, the process of gradually facing your phobia in real life. Your therapist will help you to construct a hierarchy for facing your particular fear, similar to the one you used for imagery desensitization in the previous session. You will learn a number of important ideas that are critical to your success with exposure therapy, such as learning how to retreat, the importance of taking risks and tolerating some anxiety, the importance of practicing exposure regularly, and how to handle inevitable setbacks that will occur. This is an important session; make sure you understand all of the information to follow as well as you can. If anything is unclear, ask your therapist for assistance.

Real-Life Desensitization or Exposure

Real-life desensitization is the single most effective available treatment for phobias. While imagery desensitization is often an important prerequisite, actually facing the situations that you have been avoiding in real life is essential for recovery.

Other terms for real-life desensitization are *in vivo desensitization, exposure therapy,* or simply *exposure.* In many controlled studies, direct exposure to phobic situations has consistently been found to be more effective than other, nonbehavioral treatments such as insight therapy, cognitive therapy by itself, or medication. Nothing works better for overcoming a fear than facing it—especially when this is done systematically and in small increments. Improvement resulting from real-life exposure does not disappear weeks or months later. Once you've fully desensitized yourself to a phobic situation in real life, you can remain free of fear.

For all its effectiveness, exposure isn't always a particularly easy or comfortable process to go through. Not everyone is willing to tolerate the unpleasantness of facing phobic situations or to persist with practicing real-life desensitization on a regular basis. *Exposure therapy demands a strong commitment on your part.* If you're genuinely committed to your recovery, then you'll be willing to:

- Take the risk to face your phobic situation

- *Tolerate the initial discomfort* that entering your phobic situation—even in small increments—sometimes involves

- *Persist in practicing* exposure on a consistent basis, despite probable setbacks, over a long enough period of time to overcome your fear

If you're ready to make a genuine commitment to exposure, you will very likely recover from your phobia.

The basic procedure for exposure is essentially the same as for imagery desensitization, with a few modifications, particularly involving your hierarchy of situations and the use of a support person.

Constructing an Exposure Hierarchy

You can use the same basic hierarchy of phobic scenes you constructed for your imagery desensitization. The difference is that you will be carrying out the steps of your hierarchy in real life rather than in your imagination. So you may find you need to add some additional steps to your real-life hierarchy to make transitions from step to step easier. You may need more (and smaller) steps when you face a situation in real life than when you're visualizing it in your mind.

If some of your imagery hierarchy items can't be easily adapted to a real-life situation, modify them so they can. Consider the item: "Elevator stuck between floors." This is clearly something you can't create on demand. But you can modify it to: "Standing in the elevator where the door closes and it waits a *long* time before the elevator starts to rise." This isn't the same as being stuck between floors, but it evokes some of the same feelings.

Relying on a Support Person

It's often very helpful to rely on a person you trust (such as your spouse, partner, or a friend) to accompany you on your forays into your phobia hierarchy when you first begin the process of real-life desensitization. Your support person can provide reassurance and safety, distraction (by talking with you), encouragement to persist, and praise for your incremental successes.

Your support person should not push you. That person *should* encourage you to enter your phobic situation without running away. However, it's up to you to decide on the intensity of your exposure and to determine when you reach level 4 on the Anxiety Scale and need to temporarily back off—what we call "retreat." Your support person should not criticize your attempts or tell you to try harder. Yet it is good if she or he can identify any resistance on your part and help you to recognize whether such resistance is present. Your partner's main job is to provide encouragement and support without judging your performance. We will discuss guidelines for your support person in detail later.

Identifying Your Particular Sensitivities

As you undertake exposure, look for which particular characteristics of your phobic situation make you anxious. Some of these may correspond to the variables we discussed last week: spatial proximity, temporal proximity, duration of exposure, intensity of exposure, and degree of support. However, there may be other parameters unique to your particular phobia. For example, if driving freeways is a problem, the amount of traffic or lane you're in may affect your anxiety level. Becoming aware of the specific elements of your phobic situation that make you anxious will increase your sense of control over that situation and accelerate desensitization. You may want to make a list of your particular sensitivities for your phobia on the back of your hierarchy worksheet for that phobia.

Procedure for Exposure

It is important to follow these steps when you practice exposure to your phobic situation:

1. *Proceed into your phobic situation* (whatever step in your hierarchy you're on) *and stay there so long as your anxiety stays below level 4 on the Anxiety Scale.* In other words, keep going into or remain in the situation for at least one minute or to the point where your anxiety *first begins to feel unmanageable.* If you can stay in the situation for two or three minutes, so much the better. While in the situation, use your anxiety management skills (abdominal breathing, coping statements, talking to your support person) to manage your anxiety. Even if you are *uncomfortable* in the situation, *stay with it* as long as your anxiety level does not go beyond moderate anxiety—level 3.

    If your anxiety does not go above a level 3 after two or three minutes, proceed to the next step up in your hierarchy. Then repeat step 1, staying in the situation for at least one minute or until your anxiety reaches level 4 on the Anxiety Scale. If your anxiety stays below level 4 for two to three minutes and you feel in control, proceed to the next step up in your hierarchy. Continue in this fashion for *up to an hour.* Longer exposure practice periods (i.e. one hour) are generally more effective than shorter periods. You do not need to follow steps 2 through 5 so long as your anxiety stays manageable—below level 4.

    Please Note: If your anxiety reaches or exceeds level 4 on the Anxiety Scale and you are *not* able to immediately retreat from the situation, practice your anxiety management skills (i.e., abdominal breathing, coping statements, talking to your support person, moving around if feasible) until retreat becomes possible. (If aboard an airplane, you need to reframe the idea of "retreat." Think of it as retreating to "a safe place in your mind." Realize that just as anxiety is created in your mind, so too can a sense of safety or safe place be created in your mind. Alternatively, try retreating to the rest room in the back of the plane.)

2. *Retreat*, temporarily, from the situation at any time where your anxiety reaches level 4 or *the point where it begins to feel not fully manageable*—the point where it feels like it might get out of control. Retreat means *temporarily* leaving the situation until you feel better and then *returning*. In most situations this is literally possible (when aboard an airplane, you can retreat to the rest room or to your peaceful scene in your mind). *Retreat is not the same as escaping or avoiding the situation.* It is designed to prevent you from "flooding" and risking the possibility of resensitizing yourself to the situation, which might reinforce the strength of your phobia.

3. *Recover.* After you temporarily pull back from your phobic situation, wait until your anxiety level diminishes to no more than level 1 or 2 on the Anxiety Scale. Be sure to give yourself sufficient time for your anxiety to subside. You may find that abdominal breathing or walking around at this point helps you recover your equanimity.

4. *Repeat.* After recovering, it is important to reenter your phobic situation and continue to stay with it so long as your anxiety remains below level 4 on the Anxiety Scale. Use your anxiety-management skills, as before. If you are able to go further or stay longer in the situation than you did be-fore, fine. If not—or if you can't go even as far as you did the first time—that's fine, too. Do not chastise yourself if your performance after retreating turns out to be less spectacular than it was initially. This is a common experience. In a day or two you'll find that you'll be able to continue in your progression up your hierarchy.

5. *Continue going through the above cycle—Expose-Retreat-Recover-Repeat—*until you begin to feel tired or bored, then stop for the day. This constitutes one practice session, and it will typically take you from thirty minutes to two hours. For most people an hour-long practice session per day is enough. In your first session you may be unable to master the first step in your hierarchy or you may progress through the first four or five steps. *The limit for how far you go in any practice session should be determined by the point when your anxiety reaches level 4 on the Anxiety Scale.*

    On some days you'll enjoy excellent progress, on others you'll hardly progress at all, and on still others you will not go as far as you did on preceding days. On a given Monday you might be able to ride an elevator up one floor. On Tuesday you can do the same thing but no more. Then on Wednesday you are unable to get on the elevator at all. Thursday or Friday, however, you may discover that you can go up two floors. This up-and-down, "two steps forward, one step back" phenomenon is typical of exposure therapy. Don't let it discourage you!

Guidelines for Undertaking Exposure

The following instructions are intended to help you get the most out of exposure:

1. *Be willing to take risks.*

   Entering a phobic situation that you've been avoiding for a long time is going to involve taking a mild to moderate risk. There's simply no risk-free way to face your fear and recover. Risk-taking is easier, however, when you start with small, limited goals and proceed incrementally. Establishing a hierarchy of exposures allows you to take this incremental approach.

2. *Deal with resistance.*

   Undertaking exposure to a situation that you've been avoiding may bring up resistance. Notice if you delay getting started with your exposure sessions or find reasons to procrastinate. The mere thought of actually entering your phobic situation may elicit strong anxiety, a fear of being trapped, or self-defeating statements to yourself such as, "I'll never be able to do it," or "This is hopeless." Instead of getting stuck in resistance, try to regard the process of desensitization as a major therapeutic opportunity. By plunging in you will learn about yourself and work through long-standing avoidance patterns that have held up your life. Give yourself pep talks about how much your life will improve when you are no longer held back by your phobia.

   Once you get through any initial resistance to real-life exposure, the going gets easier. If you have problems with resistance, discuss it with your therapist next time.

3. *Be willing to tolerate some discomfort.*

   Facing a situation that you've been avoiding for a long time is not particularly comfortable or pleasant. It's inevitable and, in fact, necessary that you experience some anxiety in the course of becoming desensitized. It is common to feel *worse initially* at the outset of exposure therapy before you feel better. Recognize that feeling worse is *not* an indication of regression but rather that exposure is really *working*. Feeling worse means that you're laying the foundation to feel better. As you gain more skill in handling symptoms of anxiety when they come up during exposure, your practice sessions will become easier and you'll gain more confidence about following through to completion.

   You may find the following affirmation helpful when you feel anxious: "This anxiety (or discomfort) means I'm already beginning to desensitize," or "Anxiety means that desensitization is in progress."

4. *Avoid flooding—be willing to retreat.*

   Your exposure sessions are entirely different from occasions where you are forced to be in your phobic situation. In the process of exposure, you are in control of the intensity and length of time you confront the situation—circumstance does not offer this luxury. Always be willing to retreat from a practice situation if your anxiety reaches level 4 on the Anxiety Scale. Then wait until you recover before confronting your phobic situation again. *Retreat is not cowardly*—it is the most efficient and expedient way to master a phobia. Overexposure or *flooding* may resensitize you to a situation and ultimately prolong the time it takes to overcome your phobia.

5. *Refine your hierarchy, if needed.*
   If you have a problem getting beyond a particular step in your hierarchy, try going back to the preceding step for your next practice session and work your way back up. For example, if you've mastered driving over a small bridge but have difficulty advancing to the next largest one, go back and repeat driving over the smaller bridge several times. The object is to get so bored with the smaller bridge that you feel a strong incentive to attempt the next step up in your hierarchy. When you do, have your support person go with you. If possible, add an intermediate step when you have difficulty advancing from one step to the next.

   If you have difficulty getting started with exposure therapy, try beginning with an even less challenging step than your original first step. For example, you might have a phobia about flying and you don't feel ready even to drive to the airport. As a preliminary step, watch a video that shows jets taking off and in flight, or get used to looking at photos of planes in a magazine. If you still can't make it to the airport, drive *by* it repeatedly until you feel able to drive to the airport parking lot, turn around, and return home.

6. *Plan "escape routes."*
   Suppose you're practicing on an elevator and the worst happens—it stops between floors. Or suppose you are beginning to drive on the freeway and you start to panic when you're far away from an exit. It's good to plan ahead for worst-case scenarios whenever possible. In the first example, give yourself some insurance by practicing on an elevator that has a functioning emergency phone. Or in the case of the freeway, tell yourself in advance that it will be all right to retreat to the shoulder or at least drive slowly with your emergency flashers on until you reach an exit. *Be aware of your escape routes or "trap doors" in advance of exposure to your phobia.* Knowing that you have an escape route will help make exposure easier.

7. *Trust your own pace.*
   It's important not to regard real-life exposure as some kind of race. The goal is not to see how fast you can overcome your problem: pressuring yourself to make great strides quickly is generally not a good idea. In fact doing so carries a risk of resensitizing yourself to your phobia if you attempt advanced steps in your hierarchy before becoming fully comfortable with earlier steps. Decide on the pace you wish to adopt in exposing yourself to a difficult situation, realizing that very small gains count for a lot in this type of work.

8. *Reward yourself for your successes.*
   It's common for people going through exposure to castigate themselves for not making sufficiently rapid progress. Bear in mind that it's important to

consistently reward yourself for your successes, however small. For example, being able to go into your phobic situation further than the day before is worthy of giving yourself a reward, such as a new piece of clothing or dinner out. So is being able to stay in the situation a few moments longer—or being able to tolerate anxious feelings a few moments longer. Rewarding yourself for your successes will help sustain your motivation to keep practicing. After a while your successes may become inherently rewarding.

9. *Use anxiety management strategies.*
   Whenever anxiety begins to come on, use the anxiety-management skills you have been practicing:

   - Abdominal breathing

   - Coping statements (use your list or three-by-five cards)

   - Moving around

   - Conversation with your support person

   - Distractions (such as counting the number of red cars on the freeway)

   - Anger (get angry with your anxiety)

   Remember to maintain an overall attitude of "acceptance" and "going with" any uncomfortable body sensations rather than balking or resisting them. Using abdominal breathing and coping statements in combination often helps.

10. *Practice regularly.*
    Methodical and regular practice—rather than hurrying or pressuring yourself—will do the most to expedite overcoming your fear. Ideally it is good to practice real-life exposure *three to five times per week.* Longer practice sessions, with several trials of exposure to your phobic situation, tend to be more effective than briefer sessions. As long as you retreat when appropriate, it's impossible to undergo too much exposure in a given practice session (the worst that can happen is that you might end up somewhat tired or drained).
       The *regularity* of your practice will determine the rate of your recovery. If you find it difficult to practice regularly, talk with your therapist about what kinds of resistance or other issues might be getting in your way. *Regular practice of exposure is the key to getting over your phobia.* It is the strongest predictor of your eventual success with exposure.

11. *Expect and know how to handle setbacks.*
    Not being able to tolerate as much exposure to a situation as you did previously is a normal part of recovery. Recovery simply doesn't proceed in a linear fashion—there will be plateaus and regressions as well as times of moving forward. *Setbacks are an integral part of the recovery process.*
       For example, suppose you are working on overcoming a phobia about driving on the freeway. Your practice sessions over a four-week period might go like this:

Week 1: During three out of five practice sessions you can drive the distance of one exit on the freeway.

Week 2: For five out of five practice sessions you can't get on the freeway at all. (This degree of regression is not at all uncommon.)

Week 3: For two out of five practice sessions you are able to drive the distance of one exit. During two other sessions you're able to drive the distance of two exits. One day you can't get on the freeway at all.

Week 4: Due to illness you only get in two practice sessions. On one of those days you're able to manage three exists, on the other day you go one exit.

It's very important not to let a setback discourage you from further practice. Simply chalk it up to a bad day or bad week and learn from it. Nothing can take away the progress you've made up to that point. You can use each setback as a learning experience to tell you more about how to best proceed in mastering your phobic situation. *Your ability to tolerate setbacks and still persist with your daily practice sessions is a crucial determinant of your success.*

12. *Follow through to completion.*
Finishing exposure means that you reach a point where you no longer avoid your phobic situation *and* are not afraid of anxiety whenever you confront that situation. You will need to keep exposing to the situation many times to reach a point where you're no longer anxious there. It is important not to stop short of this, not to give up before you are essentially free of anxiety in the situation. If you master your phobia to this level, you'll be unlikely to have it come up again in the future.

Homework

1. Review the section "Procedure for Exposure" so that you're thoroughly familiar with the correct procedure for real-life desensitization. Learning to retreat and recover when your anxiety reaches level 4 on the Anxiety Scale is especially important.

2. Review the section "Guidelines for Undertaking Exposure" so that you fully understand all of the ingredients that contribute to success with real-life desensitization. Your willingness to deal with initial resistance, tolerate some discomfort, learn to retreat, practice regularly, and handle setbacks is particularly important.

3. Find a relative or friend who is willing to work with you as a support person. Bring them to the following session. (**Note:** If neither a friend or relative is available, you may need to hire someone.)

4. Continue working up your imagery desensitization hierarchy, practicing at least three times this week (unless you have already completed it).

5. Continue working with abdominal breathing and progressive muscle relaxation on a daily basis. Practice your anxiety and worry management skills as needed. Reframe negative self-talk using the Worry Worksheet if anticipatory anxiety becomes particularly bothersome.

Session 7

Beginning Exposure

In this session you will begin to take initial steps toward facing your phobic situation in real life. Your therapist may accompany you on a brief initial exposure outside the consultation office. Or, if this is impractical, your therapist will instruct a support person—a friend or relative you bring with you to the session—on how to accompany you through the early stages of exposure. Whether your therapist or a support person goes with you, you'll decide how far and for how long you wish to enter into your phobic situation. You only need to be willing to take a small risk and to make an initial effort to begin facing your fear. It is your therapist or support person's responsibility to encourage you to undertake exposure without pressuring you to do more than you feel ready to. It's also important for you to let them know if your anxiety reaches level 4 on the Anxiety Scale, so that both of you know it is time to retreat. As you begin to practice exposure, watch out for your *own* tendency to try to push too hard. You may at first feel reluctant to stop and temporarily withdraw from the situation. Yet it is *always* best to retreat when your anxiety starts to feel like it might get out of control. That way you minimize the risk of having a panic attack and setting yourself back in the process of exposure. *When in doubt, always retreat and then return to the situation.* Many overenthusiastic individuals have had to learn to retreat the hard way—after experiencing one or more panic attacks during exposure. This is entirely unnecessary.

At first you will probably keep your exposure sessions short, no more than a half-hour. With experience, you may want to extend the time you practice—particularly your homework practice periods outside of therapy—up to an hour or longer. Longer exposure practice periods, with as many retreats as you need, tend to be more productive than short practices. However, don't push yourself if you're starting to feel very tired.

Remember that not all of your practice sessions will be the same. On some days you may surprise yourself how far (or how long) you can go, moving up several levels on your hierarchy. Other days you may only make a small gain or none at all. You will even have days where you can't go as far as you did on previous days. This is perfectly normal; be willing to accept that progress will not always be forward. Setbacks and temporary regressions are part of the process. If you make a commitment to practice regularly—three to five times per week—the overall direction of your practice will be forward. At times exposure may seem like hard work; however, the reward of your effort will be lasting freedom from your phobia. Through perseverance, you will attain your goal.

In this session your therapist will give you a set of guidelines to assist your support person in working with you. These guidelines are reproduced below. It would be useful to have any close friends or family members read these guidelines so that they can better appreciate what is involved in undertaking exposure therapy to overcome a phobia.

Guidelines for The Support Person

1. Be familiar with the process of exposure in overcoming phobias. See session 6 of this manual.

2. Before beginning a practice session, communicate clearly with your phobic partner about what they expect of you during practice. Do they want you to talk a lot to them? Stay right with them? Follow behind them? Wait outside? Hold their hand?

3. If your partner is easily overwhelmed, help them to break exposure down into small, incremental steps.

4. It's up to the phobic—not the support person—to define the goals of a given practice session. As a support person, be encouraging and cooperative rather than assuming the initiative.

5. Be familiar with the phobic's early warning signs of anxiety. Encourage them to *verbalize when they're beginning to feel overly anxious* (reaching level 4 on the Anxiety Scale). Don't be afraid to ask them from time to time how they're doing.

6. Be familiar with your partner's coping statements and other anxiety-management procedures. Remind them to use these techniques during exposure.

7. Don't allow your partner's distress to rattle you, but don't fail to take it seriously. Remember that anxiety isn't necessarily rational. In case of a full-blown panic attack, quietly lead your partner away from the threatening situation, end the practice session for the day, and take them home. Above all, stay close by until the panic completely subsides.

8. A hug can go much further than a lot of words. If you see that your partner is frightened in a particular situation, your hug or the offer of your hand will help relieve anxiety better than any lecture about how there is no reason to be afraid.

9. Be reliable. Be where you say you're going to be during a practice session. Don't move to another location because you want to test your partner. It can be very frightening for the phobic to return to a prearranged meeting place and find you gone.

10. *Don't push a person with phobias!* Phobics know what's going on in their body and may panic if pushed further than they're ready to go at a particular point in exposure.

11. On the other hand, encourage your partner to make the most out of practice. It's better to attempt to enter a frightening situation and have to retreat than not to try at all. Your partner's resistance may be making practice impossible or may be impeding progress. If your partner seems stalled or unmotivated to practice, ask what is getting in the way of proceeding. Assist, if you can, in exploring and identifying psychological resistance.

12. In spite of all your desire to help, phobics must assume responsibility for their own recovery. Be supportive and encouraging but avoid trying to step in and do it all for them. This will only undermine their confidence.

13. Try to see things from the phobic's standpoint. Things which seem insignificant to others—such as riding a bus or eating in a restaurant—may involve a great deal of work and courage for the phobic to achieve, even for a short period of time. These accomplishments and the efforts leading to them should be recognized.

14. Phobics generally are very sensitive and respond well to praise, even for small achievements. Praise them for whatever they accomplish and be understanding and accepting when they regress.

15. Encourage practice with rewards. For example, you might say, "When you can handle restaurants, let's have lunch together somewhere special."

16. Accept the phobic's "bad" day and reinforce the idea that they can't have a perfect day every time. Backsliding and setbacks are part of the normal course of exposure therapy.

17. It may be necessary to readjust your own schedule to effectively help your partner. Be sure you're willing to make a commitment to work with your partner regularly over a sustained period of time before offering to be a support person. If you're unable to see them through the full period of recovery (which can take several months or longer), let them know specifically how long a commitment you can make.

18. Know your own limits. Be forgiving when you are a less than perfect support person. If your capacity to be supportive has been stretched to the limit, take a break.

Homework

1. Practice real-life exposure in an effort to reach the assigned goal that you and your therapist agree on for next week. This goal is defined in terms of a particular level in your hierarchy. Practice a minimum of three times for up to an hour each time during the week, preferably more.

2. Utilize anxiety management skills (breathing, coping statements, etc.) both during as well as between exposure practice sessions, whenever physical symptoms of anxiety arise. Continue to use worry-management techniques to handle anticipatory anxiety (worry).

3. Identify, challenge, and counter negative self-talk around facing your phobia at least once during the week using the Worry Worksheet.

4. Continue progressive muscle relaxation and imagery desensitization if unfinished with your imagery hierarchy.

Evaluate Any Obstacles to Exposure/Continue Practice

In this session you and your therapist may continue to practice exposure. If this is impractical, the therapy hour will be spent 1) discussing how your initial exposure practice sessions went, 2) "troubleshooting" any problems that came up, and/or 3) exploring any resistance you may have had to doing exposure. It is important to carefully examine any obstacles that interfere with practicing exposure. You can usually overcome them with the help of your therapist. Be mindful whether any of the following types of obstacles apply in your case:

Resistance

Resistance is usually evident when you procrastinate in doing regular exposure sessions at home. Statements such as "I'm not in the mood," "I just didn't feel like it," "I'll do it next time (later, tomorrow, etc.)" are common.

Instead of chastising yourself, simply acknowledge that it *is* difficult to undertake exposure. After all, you have been avoiding your phobic situation for a long time. In facing it, you risk having anxiety come up. In fact, some anxiety is inevitable in undertaking exposure. This anxiety can be minimized by breaking the task of exposure down into a number of manageable steps and working with a support person. Even so, it is likely you may have some anxiety. Exposure is not a comfortable process; it is hard work. The reward of doing that work is that you overcome your phobia. You have to decide whether the prospect of being free of your phobia is important enough to justify putting in the work and experiencing the discomfort that's involved. Your therapist will help you in every way possible, but ultimately the decision is up to you. Undertaking exposure—facing what you fear—is the only way you're likely to overcome it.

High Anxiety

Suppose you've begun exposure, but experience high anxiety or panic from the very beginning. You may want to:

- Break down the first step of your hierarchy into two or more smaller steps. For example, instead of getting on board the elevator, repeat walking up and merely looking at an elevator many times. Instead of going to the airport terminal, drive by it a number of times.

- Spend the first few exposure sessions doing nothing other than retreating and returning. Enter your phobic situation to a very minimal degree for a short time, then back off and relax. When you've recovered, repeat the minimal exposure, followed by retreat. After an hour of small exposures alternating with retreats, you may be ready to increase the extent or duration of your exposure.

- If neither of these adjustments to the procedure work, consider taking a low dose of a benzodiazepine tranquilizer. Do this with the approval of your doctor, and *only* when undertaking exposure. A low dose (for example 0.25 mg Xanax or Klonopin) is necessary because you don't want to mask anxiety altogether during exposure. It's necessary to feel some anxiety for desensitization to occur.

Difficulty Progressing

If you're having trouble moving past a particular step, add an intermediate step, if possible. For example, if you watched someone else get an injection but are not ready to get one yourself, have the nurse let you handle (or take home) a syringe so that you can practice putting the needle up to your skin on your own (preferably without puncturing the skin).

If an intermediate step is not possible, then wait until the "right" day to attempt the next step in your hierarchy. For example, suppose you are trying to progress in exposure to driving across a longer bridge, and the increase in length or height of the next bridge seems too great. Wait until you feel highly motivated to attempt the larger bridge. Ordinarily, it is important *not* to delay exposure practice until you feel like it. You will desensitize more effectively if you resolve to practice three times per week regardless of how you are feeling. However, in moving up a difficult step in your hierarchy, it may be advisable to wait until you feel motivated to attempt it (with your support person). An alternative approach is to rely on medication, as described previously.

Setbacks

The prospect of setbacks during exposure has already been mentioned, but what was said bears repeating.

First, setbacks are normal. They happen to *everyone* undertaking exposure. The course of exposure is hardly ever linear; it is fraught with ups and downs—two steps forward, one step back. The fact that you had a setback means you are actually practicing exposure and making headway.

Second, setbacks are always temporary, provided you resolve to go forward. You do *not* lose the ground you've gained prior to the setback—it may just seem like that temporarily. When the setback passes, you will resume from where you left off in a short time if you keep practicing.

Third, it is important to view any setback not as a defeat but as an opportunity to learn. When you understand the circumstances that caused the setback, you may be able to avoid repeating those circumstances in the future. The greatest opportunity afforded by a setback is the chance to build confidence in mastering your fear. Nothing builds confidence like being able to pass through a setback and continue on your way toward your goal. However discouraging a setback may seem initially, it is always an opportunity to gain strength and confidence in your eventual success.

Secondary Gains

Secondary gains are unconscious reasons you might want to hold on to your phobia. This idea may at first seem preposterous. You protest that you want nothing more than to be free of your fear. Certainly you believe you did not develop your phobia in order to gain some hidden benefit.

Most likely your phobia did not develop out of a desire to meet some unconscious need. However, once you have the phobia, it *may* offer certain benefits or fulfill some needs. The gain you receive did not motivate or cause the phobia, it is *secondary* to it. For example, if being phobic of driving means your spouse has to take over all of your children's transportation needs, you may be relieved of something you would prefer not to do even if you could drive. The benefits of not driving may subtly interfere with your progress toward regaining that capacity.

Another secondary gain is being able to avoid the unknown. On an unconscious level, you may be so familiar with the restrictions caused by your phobia that the idea of being totally free of them is a bit scary. The "terrible known" is more comfortable than an unknown that promises to be better.

If you believe there might be secondary gains interfering with your progress in exposure, it is important to examine what they might be. Even if it initially seems ridiculous, take some time to really think about what benefits or advantages you might get from keeping your phobia. Is there anything you would be giving up if you were completely free of your fear? Then reflect about this not only for yourself but for your spouse and immediate family. Are *they* getting any benefits by your remaining phobic? How would it affect them if you were free of your fear?

Your ability to completely overcome your phobia will be enhanced by both your awareness and willingness to relinquish any secondary gains.

Homework

For this week, homework includes:

1. Practice exposure (with your support person or alone) at least three separate times during the week. Aim for the goal that you and your therapist agree upon, defined as a particular level in your hierarchy.

2. Utilize anxiety and worry management skills in advance of and during exposure practices.

3. Identify, challenge, and counter negative self-statements contributing to anticipatory anxiety at least once during the week, preferably at a time when you are relaxed and can think through the process clearly.

4. If you are experiencing resistance to exposure, explore the reasons for your resistance on your own and then with your therapist.

Session 9

Prepare for Therapy Completion/Continue Practice

The first order of business in this session is to evaluate how you are doing with exposure. As in the previous session, your therapist will assist you to work through any possible obstacles that may have come up.

You and your therapist will also decide whether it is useful to continue therapy beyond ten sessions. If your insurance or personal resources allow for this, it may be appropriate to continue with therapy for up to fifteen to twenty sessions. One reason for continuing therapy is if your therapist is accompanying you during real-life exposure. Three weeks of practice (i.e., sessions 7–9) may be insufficient to progress up through your hierarchy. In fact, in most cases you will need more than three weeks to fully master your phobia. Another reason for extending therapy may be to address personality or interpersonal issues that are interfering with your progress. For example, you may need to work through feelings around a traumatic experience with flying or driving that left you phobic. On the other hand, if your spouse is afraid of your becoming independent to the point where you can make flights alone or pass your professional exam, a few sessions of marital therapy may be needed.

If your insurance or personal resources do not permit you to continue past ten therapy sessions, your therapist will help you to plan how to continue your exposure practice on your own. In many cases your therapist will arrange for a follow-up session one or two months after the tenth session to evaluate your overall progress. Also, your therapist can be available to you by phone should you encounter problems or obstacles to successful completion of your phobia hierarchy. Your therapist's responsibility is to support you until you reach your goal, whether it is full mastery or simply coping more ably with your phobia.

When the above issues can be addressed briefly, you and your therapist may have time to practice exposure outside the office during the ninth session.

Homework

Homework for this week includes:

1. Continue to practice exposure (with your support person or alone) at least three times during the week.

2. Utilize anxiety management skills both in advance of and during exposure practices.

3. Identify, challenge, and counter any negative self-talk contributing to anticipatory anxiety at least once during the week. As in the preceding week, this should be done at a time when you are relaxed and can think through the process clearly.

4. If you are not continuing with therapy past the tenth session, make sure you and your therapist have made arrangements for you to obtain post-therapy follow-up and support, as needed. Also, be sure your support person is available to keep working with you as long as necessary.

Session 10

Final Session

Perhaps this is your final session. If so, the session will focus on three themes: 1) summarizing your progress to date, 2) discussing strategies for relapse prevention, and 3) achieving closure.

You and your therapist will discuss your progress up to this point, and you'll complete the Fear Assessment (page 71) and the Program Satisfaction Questionnaire (page 72). Are you satisfied with your progress? Are you satisfied with the therapy in general—or is there something you wish had happened that didn't? Are you willing to make a commitment following the final therapy session to continue with exposure until you reach your goal? Would you like to be able to call your therapist to report progress or any obstacles that arise? Would you like to have a follow-up session in one or two months?

There are two things to be aware of in minimizing the prospect of relapse following therapy. First, be aware of any resistance to doing regular exposure practice that may occur when you don't have the support of weekly therapy sessions. It's important to notice any procrastination or delay in getting started with exposure practice sessions—the proverbial "I'll do it tomorrow." If this gets to be a problem, be willing to work it through with your support person or else call your therapist. Second, be aware that to fully master your phobic situation, all supports need eventually to be relinquished. It is your support person that is usually the first to go; exposure isn't complete until you can handle your previously avoided situation alone. Each hierarchy step that was handled with the help of a support person needs to be negotiated alone.

A good way to wean yourself away from your support person is to attempt early steps in your hierarchy alone while negotiating more advanced steps (i.e., the last three or four steps) with your support person. In short, you would practice in the weeks following therapy at two different points in your hierarchy, one with support and the other alone. If your hierarchy has twelve steps, you might begin trying out steps 1 or 2 alone by the time you've reached steps 8 or 9 with support. For example, if you have reached the point where you can ride an elevator to the fortieth floor of a sixty-floor building with your support person, you need to begin working on the first two or three floors alone. If this is too demanding, you might phase out reliance on your support person as follows: 1) your support person waits at the second floor while you ride the elevator alone, 2) your support person waits at the ground level while you ascend to the second floor and return, and 3) your support person waits in a car outside the building. Similarly, for a fear of driving freeways, your support person might: 1) follow in a second car, 2) follow a few hundred yards behind in a second car, 3) wait at the destination, 4) wait at the point of origin, and 5) be available by cellular phone. By the time you have successfully negotiated the highest and last step of your hierarchy with support, you should be well on your way to progressing up the earlier steps on your own. You are not finished with exposure until you can progress up through all of the steps in your hierarchy alone. This goal is almost always attainable with enough practice.

Beyond your support person are all the other types of supports that can assist exposure in the early stages, including medications, cellular phones, lucky charms, and various distraction techniques. If you need to rely on such "safety signals" indefinitely to handle your phobic situation, you may run the risk of having anxiety crop up should you ever be suddenly faced with the situation without such devices being available. Relying on supports to handle a phobia is all right if all you desire is to cope well. However, full mastery of a phobia, with minimal risk of relapse, requires facing the situation repeatedly without supports.

A final important consideration in minimizing relapse is that you continue to practice all of the anxiety and worry management techniques you have learned, particularly abdominal breathing and the use of coping statements. This is necessary both at the time of practicing exposure as well as at other times when anticipatory anxiety (worry) comes up. Following through with exposure to completion is ultimately the best way to dispense with anticipatory anxiety about facing your fear.

When you and your therapist have finished discussing the importance of completing exposure as well as how to minimize the prospect of relapse, it is time to bring therapy to a close. You and your therapist will talk about any feelings that come up around having to end the therapy. This is unlikely to be your final contact with your therapist, since arrangements for a follow-up session and/or continuing support by phone are already in place.

Further Reading

Beck, Aaron T., and Gary Emery. 1981. *Anxiety Disorders and Phobias: A Cognitive Perspective.* New York: Basic Books.

Bourne, Edmund. 1995. *The Anxiety and Phobia Workbook*, 2nd ed. Oakland: New Harbinger Publications. (See especially chapters 1, 4, 7 and 8.)

McKay, Matthew, and Patrick Fanning. 1997. *Thoughts and Feelings*, 2nd ed. Oakland: New Harbinger Publications.

Fear Questionnaire

In regard to your phobia, choose a number from the scale below to show how much you are troubled by each problem listed, and write the number in the blank.

0	1	2	3	4	5	6	7	8
Hardly at all		Slightly troublesome		Definitely troublesome		Markedly troublesome		Very severely troublesome

_____ 1. Feeling miserable or depressed

_____ 2. Feeling irritable or angry

_____ 3. Feeling tense or panicky

_____ 4. Upsetting thoughts coming into your mind

_____ 5. Feeling you or your surroundings are strange or unreal

_____ 6. Other feelings (describe)

7. How would you rate the present state of your phobic symptoms on the scale below? Please circle one number between 0 and 8.

0	1	2	3	4	5	6	7	8
No phobias present		Slightly disturbing/ not really disturbing		Definitely disturbing/ disabling		Markedly disturbing/ disabling		Very severely disturbing/ disabling

Adapted from the "Fear Questionnaire" by I. M. Marks and A. M. Matthews, 1978.

Program Satisfaction Questionnaire (PSQ)

Please evaluate the therapy program you have just completed by answering the following questions. Circle the number that best reflects your opinion. Your honest answer, whether positive or negative, will give us feedback to make the program better.

1. How effective was the therapy program in helping you with your problem?

       1   2   3   4   5   6   7

Not effective   *Moderately effective*   *Extremely effective*

2. How helpful were the homework and exercises in this therapy program?

       1   2   3   4   5   6   7

Not helpful   *Moderately helpful*   *Extremely helpful*

3. Were the skills you learned in this therapy program useful for coping with your problem?

       1   2   3   4   5   6   7

Not useful   *Moderately useful*   *Extremely useful*

4. Overall, how would you rate the quality of this therapy?

       1   2   3   4   5   6   7

High quality   *Moderate quality*   *Low quality*

5. If someone with a similar problem to yours asked for recommendations, how would you describe the usefulness of this therapy program?

       1   2   3   4   5   6   7

Not useful   *Moderately useful*   *Extremely useful*

6. If you could go back to remake your decision about this therapy program, would you do it again?

       1   2   3   4   5   6   7

No definitely   *Uncertain*   *Yes definitely*

7. How successfully were your goals met by this therapy program?

       1   2   3   4   5   6   7

Goals met   *Moderately successful*   *Goals not met*
                         with goals

8. How would you rate your improvement in the symptoms that concerned you most?

       1   2   3   4   5   6   7

Extremely improved   *Moderately improved*   *Not improved*

Edmund Bourne, Ph.D., has specialized in treating anxiety disorders and related problems for almost two decades. He is author of the highly regarded *Anxiety & Phobia Workbook*, which has helped numerous people in the United States and other countries. For many years, Dr. Bourne was director of The Anxiety Treatment Center in San Jose and Santa Rosa, California. Currently he resides in Kona, Hawaii and in California.

Linda K. Collevecchio, PhD, LLC

Some Other New Harbinger Self-Help Titles

Dr. Carl Robinson's Basic Baby Care, $10.95
Better Boundries: Owning and Treasuring Your Life, $13.95
Goodbye Good Girl, $12.95
Being, Belonging, Doing, $10.95
Thoughts & Feelings, Second Edition, $18.95
Depression: How It Happens, How It's Healed, $14.95
Trust After Trauma, $13.95
The Chemotherapy & Radiation Survival Guide, Second Edition, $13.95
Heart Therapy, $13.95
Surviving Childhood Cancer, $12.95
The Headache & Neck Pain Workbook, $14.95
Perimenopause, $13.95
The Self-Forgiveness Handbook, $12.95
A Woman's Guide to Overcoming Sexual Fear and Pain, $14.95
Mind Over Malignancy, $12.95
Treating Panic Disorder and Agoraphobia, $44.95
Scarred Soul, $13.95
The Angry Heart, $13.95
Don't Take It Personally, $12.95
Becoming a Wise Parent For Your Grown Child, $12.95
Clear Your Past, Change Your Future, $12.95
Preparing for Surgery, $17.95
Coming Out Everyday, $13.95
Ten Things Every Parent Needs to Know, $12.95
The Power of Two, $12.95
It's Not OK Anymore, $13.95
The Daily Relaxer, $12.95
The Body Image Workbook, $17.95
Living with ADD, $17.95
Taking the Anxiety Out of Taking Tests, $12.95
The Taking Charge of Menopause Workbook, $17.95
Living with Angina, $12.95
Five Weeks to Healing Stress: The Wellness Option, $17.95
Choosing to Live: How to Defeat Suicide Through Cognitive Therapy, $12.95
Why Children Misbehave and What to Do About It, $14.95
When Anger Hurts Your Kids, $12.95
The Addiction Workbook, $17.95
The Mother's Survival Guide to Recovery, $12.95
The Chronic Pain Control Workbook, Second Edition, $17.95
Fibromyalgia & Chronic Myofascial Pain Syndrome, $19.95
Flying Without Fear, $12.95
Kid Cooperation: How to Stop Yelling, Nagging & Pleading and Get Kids to Cooperate, $12.95
The Stop Smoking Workbook: Your Guide to Healthy Quitting, $17.95
Conquering Carpal Tunnel Syndrome and Other Repetitive Strain Injuries, $17.95
Wellness at Work: Building Resilience for Job Stress, $17.95
An End to Panic: Breakthrough Techniques for Overcoming Panic Disorder, Second Edition, $17.95
Living Without Procrastination: How to Stop Postponing Your Life, $12.95
Goodbye Mother, Hello Woman: Reweaving the Daughter Mother Relationship, $14.95
Letting Go of Anger: The 10 Most Common Anger Styles and What to Do About Them, $12.95
Messages: The Communication Skills Workbook, Second Edition, $13.95
Coping With Chronic Fatigue Syndrome: Nine Things You Can Do, $12.95
The Anxiety & Phobia Workbook, Second Edition, $17.95
The Relaxation & Stress Reduction Workbook, Fourth Edition, $17.95
Living Without Depression & Manic Depression: A Workbook for Maintaining Mood Stability, $17.95
Coping With Schizophrenia: A Guide For Families, $13.95
Visualization for Change, Second Edition, $13.95
Postpartum Survival Guide, $13.95
Angry All the Time: An Emergency Guide to Anger Control, $12.95
Couple Skills: Making Your Relationship Work, $13.95
Self-Esteem, Second Edition, $13.95
I Can't Get Over It, A Handbook for Trauma Survivors, Second Edition, $15.95
Dying of Embarrassment: Help for Social Anxiety and Social Phobia, $12.95
The Depression Workbook: Living With Depression and Manic Depression, $17.95
Men & Grief: A Guide for Men Surviving the Death of a Loved One, $13.95
When the Bough Breaks: A Helping Guide for Parents of Sexually Abused Children, $11.95
When Once Is Not Enough: Help for Obsessive Compulsives, $13.95
The Three Minute Meditator, Third Edition, $12.95
Beyond Grief: A Guide for Recovering from the Death of a Loved One, $13.95
Hypnosis for Change: A Manual of Proven Techniques, Third Edition, $13.95
When Anger Hurts, $13.95

Call **toll free, 1-800-748-6273,** to order. Have your Visa or Mastercard number ready. Or send a check for the titles you want to New Harbinger Publications, Inc., 5674 Shattuck Ave., Oakland, CA 94609. Include $3.80 for the first book and 75¢ for each additional book, to cover shipping and handling. (California residents please include appropriate sales tax.) Allow two to five weeks for delivery.

Prices subject to change without notice.